shut up

CHRISTY PIERCE

WITH HELP FROM OVER 1,000 TEENS & COLLEGE STUDENTS

ISBN: 1537629107 | ISBN-13: 978-1537629100

DEDICATED TO OUR FRIENDS & HEROES

Bill, Kristin, Cole, and Reid Eberwein

———

IN MEMORY OF WALKER EBERWEIN

We love you Walker. May life come out of your death in Jesus' name.

———

Acknowledgments

X   A small army of people have helped me make this *shut up* book, website, and ministry move from being a dream to becoming a movement which is helping teens and college students all over the United States. Without the help of many teens, college students, doctors, teachers, parents, pastors, therapists, and many others, I would never have been able to finish the book. I'm deeply grateful to each of you who gave your time, energy, wisdom, finances, and personal stories. I couldn't have done it without you.

Thank you, Julie Davies, my assistant and partner in ministry. You were my constant encourager to follow God's call, and you believed in the vision before anyone else did. Your courage sharing your own story about attempting suicide has empowered other teens and college students to share their own. Our website and social media platform are awesome because of your leadership. I love you and thank God for you every day.

Many doctors, therapists, psychiatrists, and medical research specialists have helped by giving us clinically sound research and statistics about the mental health crisis among teens and college students today. Thank you, Dr. Megan Jones, for your wisdom, ideas, and for your wonderful organization, Lantern, which is helping thousands of teens and college students today. Dr. Carol Peyser, thank you for connecting us with Johns Hopkins University's new app (mADAP), which is a great resource for teens suffering from depression. I'm thankful for the staff of Crisis Text Line and the team at National Suicide Prevention for their input. To our New Hope Ministries Board, thank you for partnering with me in God's call to help hurting young people. Without your constant prayers, wisdom, and love, nothing would have happened.

To my dear friends, Dan and Pam Chun, thank you for giving me a speaking platform at the Hawaiian Islands Ministries conferences which was invaluable in connecting us with teens and college students and launching this ministry. None of this ministry would be happening without many generous donors who helped launch this *shut up* movement. Thank you for believing in God's call upon my life and for your generous hearts that have helped start up this ministry and book.

From the very beginning, we knew that this book would be lame unless God raised up hundreds of youth to help me write it. So, we got on our knees and prayed for teens and college students to join our mission. God provided above and beyond what we could have imagined! In three short years the Lord connected us with over a thousand young people. To our Hawaiian young friends, a big "mahalo" for your stories, ideas, and feedback. I am deeply touched that you call me "Auntie Christy," and I consider you friends and ohana. Huge thanks to the students and staff at The King's Academy in Sunnyvale, California for all your awesome ideas and helping with our website. Thanks to Kaitlyn, our teenage angel in Florida, who spoke God's encouragement to Benji and me about finishing this book while on an airplane. To you college students at UCLA, Pepperdine, LMU, Baylor, SLO, Berkeley, University of Georgia, University of Kansas, Mississippi State University, Stanford University, and Canada College, we are grateful for your unique perspective on anxiety and depression among college students today. I wish I could list all of the names of teens and college students who have helped us, but you know who you are, so big hugs to all of you for sharing your time, ideas, and stories.

To my wonderful editor, Jennie Bower, and to my book designer, Taylor Hanson, you guys are the best. *Shut Up* is a much better book because of your careful editing and creative design. To our intern from England, Lea, and to Noelle Chun, thank you for the hours of interviewing and filming teens and college students.

No words are enough to convey my deep respect and gratitude to our heroic friends, Bill, Kristin, Cole, and Reid Eberwein for inspiring all of us by your incredibly strong faith in Jesus despite the unthinkable tragedy of Walker's death. We will never know this side of heaven why terrible things like this happen to such beautiful, lovely people who are following God. You'll never know how many people have been impacted by your faith and love for Jesus in dark times. Because of you, life will come out of death for many young people.

Finally, thank you to my biggest cheerleaders and loving family. Corey, Annie, and Benji. You are three of the best people I know. You are kind, wise, hilarious, and you love me when I don't deserve it. Thank you for your ruthless, unedited feedback about this book and telling me the real truth about how teens are suffering today. God must really love me to let me be your mom. To my loving husband and best friend, Ben, thank you for standing with me and believing in me when I wanted to quit. I love you with all my heart, and it's my greatest honor to be your wife and partner in ministry.

Most importantly, thank you Jesus for the incredible privilege of writing this book and connecting me with thousands of amazing people along the journey. Because of you, our loving God, we can have hope that "life will come out of death" like Annie's dream prophesied. You gave your very life for all of us, that we might know joy in this life and have eternally happy lives with you in heaven. Use this book for your glory, and bring healing and new life to your children.

With gratitude and love,

Christy

Contents

Preface 1

X   Wait what? Are two prefaces really necessary for this book? Yes. I didn't realize it at first, but my three teens, Corey (16), Annie (14), and Benji (12) insisted I add this story – so, a second preface it is. Because this book isn't for older people; it's for teens and college students. I've learned something important from talking to over a thousand teens and college students: *We* don't get it. There is no way that we parents, teachers, counselors, coaches, and other adults can really understand the pressure facing your generation today. If anyone pretends that they fully understand what it's like growing up in today's world, and if anyone pretends that they have all the answers about what you should do to feel better, then they really don't have a clue what's going on today.

The truth is that the pressures, pain, and suffering around you are way bigger than most anything we as parents saw when we were your age. I overheard one young middle school girl say that her parents locked her in the garage one night because she got a B+ on a test. Seriously? In my opinion, the extreme pressure put on you (sometimes by parents, teachers, and coaches) to excel in academics, sports, drama, and everything else is crazy. Plus, parents and teachers (myself included) really don't understand how hard it is to grow up in your world. Cyber bullying, pressure to send nude selfies (and then seeing your private body parts go viral with comments about how imperfect your body is, as if anyone has a perfect body!), and pressure to do drugs are common among your generation. Throw all of this together and no wonder many of you are anxious, depressed, or hopeless about your future.

Honestly, I'm going to say some things that I know will make some adults mad at me. That's ok. My heart is broken for all your generation is going through, and it's worth the risk to tick off a few parents or teachers in the process.

Here's an embarrassing story (which just might make someone angry...). Last week, I was walking my dogs, Sam and Lizzie, in our neighborhood. As I walked past my kids' old elementary school, a mom (I'll call her Suzy) waved at me from across the street. You have to understand, Suzy drove me crazy when our kids played together in kindergarten. When her little girl was just five years old, she would brag that she was already on the club soccer team, learning French and Spanish, and was Clara in the Nutcracker ballet. Suzy would go on to say that her husband had her daughter working out with a trainer so that she didn't get fat before starting 2nd grade. If that wasn't bad enough, Suzy once told me that they got a tutor for her because she got a B in kindergarten math and that was "just unacceptable." That poor child. Every time I saw her on the playground, Lily (not her real name, of course) looked so anxious and just plain sad.

Now, fast forward to last week. As I was walking Sam and Lizzie in our neighborhood, I saw Suzy down the street and she was waving at me. I'll admit it. I tried to hide. I even stooped down and pretend-ed to pick up Lizzie's poop so this mom wouldn't stop and talk with me. Nope. Here she came, crossing the street, shouting at me,

"Christy! I've been yelling at you! Didn't you hear me? How are your kids? We haven't seen you in forever! Let me tell you about our little Lily. You just won't believe your ears! She is the student council pres-ident, and just made the varsity soccer team. She's vice president of the French club and is dancing the lead role in the ballet! Of course, her grades are suffering a bit. She was making a 4.0 in freshman year, but this year, she ended up with a B in Algebra. She won't be able to get into Stanford if she gets a B, and that's where we want her to go. My husband was so upset that he grounded her for a week." And then Suzy laughed. I think it was the laugh that got me.

In that moment, something inside me snapped. I felt this incredi-ble rage rising up inside me, and inside my head I could hear myself screaming, *SHUT THE HELL UP!* It was like an out-of-body experience, as if I was looking at myself from above, getting more and more angry, until I exploded. For a minute, I froze, and I wondered if I had actually screamed, "*SHUT THE HELL UP!*" out loud. But she was still talking and talking and talking. So, I figured that if I *had* actually said it out loud, she might be more upset. Thankfully, I had managed to keep a lid on that volcano of rage and was just shouting those words inside my mind. Finally, I couldn't stand her talking anymore, and I raised my hand up in front of her face, like a stop sign, and said,

"Suzy, I have a question for you. Did you ask Lily if she wanted to be president of the student body, president of the French club, varsi-ty soccer captain, make straight As, and be a ballerina....*all at the same time?! Does Lily want to go to Stanford or is that your dream?*" The minute the words flew out of my mouth, I knew I was in trou-ble. For the first time ever, Suzy was at a loss for words. She shut her mouth. With an angry look on her face, she spun around and marched away from me. I'm guessing that Suzy has decided she doesn't want to be my best friend. She might decide never to talk with me again. That's OK with me.

FYI, I'm not in the habit of screaming at people. I'm a pastor, a *Christian* author, and most of the time I think people would say I'm a pretty nice person. But the level of rage I was feeling was new to me, and it left me wondering why I had literally almost told another mom to *shut the hell up*. As I was stirring spaghetti sauce that night in the kitchen, the answer came to me: I realized that I have become so angry at the huge pressure on teens and college students I'm seeing today. I'm so tired of hearing stories of kids who are only sleeping five hours at night because they're frantically trying to finish homework after rushing home following a club sport's game. I'm so sad to hear the stories of teens who are depressed, anxious, cutting, or even suicidal over all this pressure.

I'm not a perfect parent (as you can clearly see from my little incident). In the next preface, I'll speak to parents and other adults and admit that I'm far from perfect and fall into the same trap at times. But I believe that it's time for us as parents, academic leaders, and coaches to seriously consider the toll all of this pressure is taking on our kids. More of us need God's eyes of compassion for those of you who feel scared, depressed, or alone with no one to listen to your feelings.

Let me be very clear and honest with you. Believe it or not, the point of this book isn't about saying shut up to other people. The actual purpose of this book is to help you know how to say shut up to the negative, lying, and dark voices that are inside your own mind. These are the thoughts that can make you feel so bad about yourself that you begin to feel anxious, depressed, lonely, hopeless, and sometimes seem to take over everything.

These thoughts can even whisper lies to you about doing stuff to harm yourself or even give up living. My hope is that by the time you finish this book, you will know which voices inside your head are from God, which are from your own pain, and which are the lying, dark voices. With God's help, you really can shut up the dark voices inside your head. You can shut them up and make them stop. You really can learn to hear God's voice of love, encouragement, and peace. You deserve that. You can be happy and have joy in your life.

I will promise you this: I won't pretend that I have all the easy answers to fix your problems. No one can do that. But I want you to know that there is hope. I believe that this book can connect you with God in a life-changing way, because the truth is only Jesus can really fully understand your private world, and He loves you more than any human ever could, including your best friend. In fact, Jesus can be your perfect best friend.

So, I hope you'll keep reading. You'll see that this book is filled with stories of teens and college students who have shared their painful stories to help others in their generation. Over the past three years, we have talked to over a thousand teens and college students, and many of them have given us their input about what might help people in your generation. They've shared their stories and ideas on our website: www.sayshutup.com. I don't think any adult, myself included, will have all the answers to help your generation. Actually, I believe that you guys are the ones with the best ideas that will actually end up helping people your age. As you read this book, if you think of things that might help teens or college students, please email, text, or call us. We would really love to hear your ideas.

But first, let me tell you why I wrote this book in the first place. It began with a tragic story, but God is using the sad story to bring hope, healing, and new life to other teens.

P.S.: If you are a parent or adult reader, this book is for teens and college students, but the next preface is written specifically for you.

Preface 2

X   If you're a parent reading this book, please know that this book isn't about bashing parents, coaches, teachers, or the other good people who are trying to help teens today. Most parents I know are doing their very best to give our kids a good life. We all want our kids to have a happy future. Obviously, I am not a perfect parent (as you can clearly see from my little outburst in our quiet neighborhood...).

Some of what I've written in this book may make some of you squirm with discomfort – and it may even offend you. I've felt all these emotions as I've learned more about the inner world of today's youth. What is happening among teens and young adults today should offend all of us. One of the reasons so many parents are pushing our kids to do well in academics, sports, or whatever else is that we feel pressure from society that this is the "right" thing to do. We live in a culture where the pressure for our kids to compete in academics, sports, music, dance, drama (...the list goes on) is huge. I know. We feel like if we don't push our kids to do these things, we will have failed them. We worry that their friends, neighbors, and classmates will pass them by, and they won't end up having a successful life. You should know that as I write this book today, I'm on my way to a varsity basketball game for my son and taking my daughter to her ballet class. We are all trying to give our kids great lives. But what the teens are telling us now, if we will listen, is that the pressure is having unintended consequences.

I am from a family of medical doctors. Consequently, publishing correct statistics is very important to me because I want to accurately present the facts given the mental health crisis we are currently seeing among today's youth. The statistics and quotes in this book have been carefully researched and come from some really respected research bodies like the Centers for Disease Control and Prevention (CDC) and the National Institute of Mental Health (NIMH), and from psychiatrists, psychologists, doctors, and therapists that I've consulted over the past three years. Sadly, it's likely that the statistics you are about to read are worsening, because that's the trend among teens and college students. Also, we know that these statistics only represent those who are reporting them (kids who have come into emergency rooms, doctor's offices, and who respond to surveys) because most teens and college students choose to stay silent when suffering.

When I started writing this book two years ago, teenage suicide was the third leading cause of death among teens age 10-24. As I'm finishing the book now (summer of 2016) the CDC's latest report shows that suicide is the second leading cause of death for youth between the ages of 10 and 24 in the United States.[1]

A nationwide survey of youth in grades nine through 12 in public and private schools in the United States found 16 percent of students seriously considering suicide, 13 percent had created a plan, and 8 percent who had actually tried to take their own life in the 12 months preceding the survey.[2] The CDC also says that approximately 157,000 youth between the ages of 10 and 24 receive medical care for self-inflicted injuries at emergency departments across the U.S.[3]

NIMH reported this:

> About 11 percent of adolescents have a depressive disorder by 18 according to the National Comorbidity Survey-Adolescent Supplement (NCS-A). Girls are more likely than boys to experience depression. The risk for depression increases as a child gets older. According to the World Health Organization, major depressive disorder is the leading cause of disability among Americans age 15-44.[4]

Teenage depression, anxiety, and suicide isn't just a problem here in the United States. Listen to what this news article had to say:

> Two teens in eastern China committed suicide after "failing to complete homework assignments" in an extreme case highlighting the immense pressure schoolchildren can face. In a highly competitive education system which emphasizes rote learning and passing exams, Chinese students spend on average 8.6 hours a day in class and can expect several more hours of assignments afterwards. A 15-year-old boy in Nanjing, the capital of Jiangsu province, who failed to finish homework from a three-day public holiday jumped to his death around 11:00 a.m. on Thursday, the China Daily said a 13-year-old boy in the same town got up at 4:00 a.m. on Thursday to complete holiday assignments but was found hanged on a staircase at his home two hours later, it said.[5]

Crazy, right? It's happening everywhere. In an article published on March 7, 2012 in *The Washington Post*, Will Englund states, "Russia has the third-highest teenage suicide rate in the world, just behind its neighbors Belarus and Kazakhstan and more than three times that of the United States. On an average day, about five Russians under age 20 take their own lives."[6]

God called me to write this *shut up* book after a 16-year-old boy named Walker jumped in front of a train and ended his life. Walker grew up in a Christian family, and I knew his family well. These friends have a deep faith in Jesus and are some of the best people you could ever meet in this life. Seeing how this could happen to such a loving family is part of how God called me into this mission of understanding society's pressure on youth and the other forces of darkness that are targeting our kids today. You'll hear more about Walker's story in the introduction (which Walker's mom helped me write).

Let me warn you ahead of time. Many of the stories in this book and statistics might shock you. They shocked me. Since 2014, we've talked to over a thousand teens and college students. Their stories would break your heart.

Previously, I worked in a clinical setting as a counselor. Right now, I'm an author, conference speaker, and pastor. My greatest joy in life is being a wife and mom of three wonderful kids who are now teen-agers. Many good people are trying to help this generation that is suffering. Psychiatrists, doctors, therapists, counselors, social work-ers, youth pastors, teachers, and parents are doing their best to raise kids in this difficult world. Despite all the help available to teens today, the epidemic of teenage depression, anxiety, drugs, bullying, cyber bullying, cutting, eating disorders, and suicide is increasing at an alarming rate.

What I can tell you is that from my experience over the past two years researching these issues, interviewing doctors, and talking with hundreds of teenagers is that the stories and statistics in this book are only the tip of a huge iceberg. If you think these problems aren't widespread among young people that you know, think again. Social media, television, and video games today bombard our teens with images of sex, porn, drugs, alcohol abuse, and violence. Young people are under more pressure than ever before. The epidemic is real.

This week I received calls from two different parents with teenagers

who were hospitalized (on suicide watch) because of stress over the SAT test. Wow. In our San Francisco Bay area, three kids committed suicide by jumping in front of a train (this month). Recently, one girl jumped off a bridge into highway traffic and died. This stuff is really happening. This is an epidemic in the Bay area. Things that never happened decades ago is now normal. (My generation rarely heard about suicide happening and now most teens know about someone who is depressed, cutting, suicidal, doing drugs, or privately suffering and telling no one.)

Some parents think that once their child reaches college, they will be safe from the problems troubling middle and high school students. But, in 2012, the American College Health Association (ACHA) conducted a nationwide survey of college students at two-and four-year institutions and found that about 30 percent of college students reported feeling "so depressed that it was difficult to function" at some time in the past year. [7]

My heart is broken as I hear their stories. My heart is also broken for the loving parents who want to help but don't know how. This book is an attempt to help us all, kids and adults together, stand against these forces and reclaim God's clear loving voice over and against all the negative stuff. I believe there is hope. For every sad story I hear, I also see amazing stories of teens and college students who are overcoming these odds to become incredible young men and women.

Let me be very clear. ***This book is not about telling parents or any person to shut up. The purpose of this book is to help your kids experience God's love in a personal way that empowers them to shut up the negative and dark voices inside their heads.*** Recently, I've been speaking to parents on this shut up topic and they always ask me the same question,

"Christy, what do you think is the cause of this mental health crisis among teens and college students today?" I tell them the same answer: I don't believe there is one cause. I believe it's a multifaceted problem with many causes including today's pressure on kids to excel in everything, coupled with new social media, and greater awareness of mental illness (all of these will be addressed in the book). However, I think there is another significant contributing factor that few people are addressing which I want to discuss as well. I believe there are forces of good and evil in the world and that spiritual warfare is a real thing, which is partially responsible (again it's multi-faceted) for the more dark horrific stories of cutting, school shootings, and the suicide epidemic we are witnessing today. These are the destructive voices that are pushing kids to do drugs, to cut themselves, to starve themselves, or even to commit suicide. Our kids are under tremendous spiritual warfare in addition to the society's pressure. This book and our www.sayshutup.com website is aimed at helping young people understand the different thoughts, voices, and messages inside their minds and empowers them to silence those dark voices with God's power. On our website, you will see videos of teens and college students telling their own stories and how they've learned to shut up the negative and dark voices in their lives. Whether you are a Christian or not, I invite you to read the stories of the many young people who have experienced healing and freedom through God's love.

Finally, this book is written specifically for young people. It's for teenagers and young adults, written with the help of over a thousand teenagers and college students. I'm honored to know these amazing young people. While this book is written for teens and college-aged students (the parent version of *shut up* is coming out soon), I would invite you to read it, so that you might better understand teens today and join the army of people God is raising up to love and help hurting teens in today's world. My prayer is that God uses this book to bring healing, hope, and freedom to these heroic young people so that they might help others suffering in their generation.

Introduction

X   October 14, 2013 was a day like any other day for most. But, for a family in northern California, it was one of the saddest days of their lives. Their son, 16-year old Walker, took his own life. Walker's journey with depression started a year prior to this event when his depressive mood took hold of his thoughts, feelings, and, ultimately, his life. It started with the onset of puberty and grabbed a hold of him until he spiraled down to the point where his family and friends could no longer reach him.

I knew Walker and his family very well. His parents are great people and committed Christians. Bill, his father, was an elder at his church. Kristin, his mother, dedicated her life to her boys. Walker's siblings, Cole and Reid, were close to him. They all tried many things and many ways to help him, yet it wasn't enough to fight back the demons that depression instilled in his psyche.

Why wasn't it enough? This might be the first question. What thoughts were going through his head to keep him beyond reach? Walker was like a baby bird in a tree with the whole family cheering him on to fly, but Walker couldn't break free and do it. He didn't fly. He couldn't fly. This baby bird, with its broken wing, fell out of the safety of the nest. His family was left at the bottom of the tree with their arms wide open, looking up, and trying to figure out why their outstretched arms couldn't reach or catch him.

Why couldn't they catch him in time? Why was he so lost? Why did he not have hope? Why did God do this to his beautiful, God-fearing family? Years prior, Bill was diagnosed with cancer. Was that the trigger for Walker's depression? Was it the onset of puberty's flood of hormones that were wreaking havoc on him? Why were their words of encouragement deflected and heard as discouragement?

Six months after Walker took his own life, Bill died of cancer. A family of five was reduced to three in six months. I was driving home from the Eberwein's house the day after Walker died, and I sensed the Spirit of God speak to me. Honestly, it was one of the clearest messages I've heard in my life. I was praying for Walker's family and I saw a dim picture in my mind of a book with the words "shut up" written on the cover. Confused, I prayed silently. God, is this you? And this is what I heard:

Christy, I want you to write this book for youth so they can understand the difference between My voice, their own pain, and the dark, destructive voices.

As I write this book, the CDC reports that suicide is the second leading cause of death among young people 10-24.[8] But if you're a young person, I'm pretty sure that you already know these stats. Most teens and young adults know way more than their parents about these problems. You guys see it firsthand. Bullying, depression, cutting, eating disorders, academic pressure, and suicidal thoughts are all around you. If you are a young person in today's world, chances are you've either had friends who suffer from these problems or you have experienced them yourself. Since 2014, we have been speaking to middle school, high school, and college students about these topics. Since that time, we have spoken to over 1,200 students and received surveys from over 350 students on specific questions related to depression, anxiety, and suicide. The majority of them (85 percent) told us that they have known someone at some point in their lives who has considered, or know someone right now who is considering, suicide. I know that many of you often suffer alone for reasons we'll talk about in this book.

Here's my sneak preview before you read this book. In chapter two, you'll hear me rant about the pressure to excel in sports and academics being put on you guys today. (Honestly, I might not be too popular among some adults after they hear me vent.) Too much homework, too many demands to be "successful" in everything from geometry to Honor's club, to sports' practices that last until 8 p.m. only to go home to study until midnight. Too many sleepless nights from anxiety over homework or other pressures. Did you know that the American Academy of Pediatrics (AAP) recommends you guys get 8.5 to 9.5 hours a sleep a night? Are you laughing? Many teens I talk with say they're getting five hours or less because they are up studying after sports or other activities that meet for hours after school. You may be sick of math homework, so I don't want to throw more statistics at you, but I think you might be encouraged to see what the "experts" are saying about how important it is for you guys to get good sleep. In fact, good doctors at the AAP are even fighting to get middle and high schools to start the day later. Here is what they say about the stress that is causing many of you to lose sleep:

Many studies have documented that the average adolescent in the U.S. is chronically sleep-deprived and pathologically sleepy. A National Sleep Foundation poll found that 59 percent of sixth through eighth graders and 87 percent of high school students in the U.S. were getting less that the recommended 8.5 to 9.5 sleep hours on a school night. [9]

That same press release quotes Dr. Judith Owens, lead author on the policy statement, as saying, "The research is clear that adolescents who get enough sleep have a reduced risk of being overweight or suffering depression, are less likely to be involved in automobile accidents, and have better grades, higher standardized test scores and an overall better quality of life." [10]

If you are a young person reading this book, I want to encourage you that you guys are doing the academic homework now that your parents did in college. The expectation is you must excel in both school and in sports (or dramas, or music, or dance – the list goes on!). I know several kids right now who are so stressed over their college applications that they're severely depressed (one is cutting and the other contemplating suicide). Wow. How crazy is that kind of pressure on a 16-year-old? (BTW: Kids are now expected to take their SATs way before they hit senior year on top of their studies. Uh, what sense does that make considering you need senior material to study for the SATs?)

I didn't write this book alone. I'm a mom with three teenage kids and they tell me what they're seeing and hearing. It breaks my heart. We share this story with those thousands of teens who have given me their wisdom to help me write this book. They were real with their pain and courageously shared their stories. Not only that, they have some great ideas. I'm convinced that you guys know more about the real issues facing your generation than your parents, teachers, doctors, therapists, and youth pastors understand. You probably have some good ideas that will help other young people in your generation.

Negative and dark thoughts can become so loud that it's hard to hear the loving voice of God. I'm not sure what you believe about God or if you've ever experienced the Spirit of God speak directly to you. You may not even believe in God. That's OK. Please read on and understand that I'm not encouraging anyone to be a religious person or having to do stuff to earn God's love. (I'm not a "religious" person myself even though I'm a pastor.) Instead, I'm a broken person who has made mistakes in life, and the loving presence of God has healed me and given me hope. This God is love. No matter what you believe, or what you've done in your life, the Spirit of God can heal you and help you experience God's very real love in a way that will change your whole life. Whatever pain you're experiencing right now can be healed, and I promise you there is hope. There is always hope.

God wants to give you and your generation spiritual power to shut up the negative messages inside your head. These may be quiet messages whispering inside your mind. (*You're ugly; you're fat; you're stupid; no one likes you; you're all alone, etc.*) You know what I mean. But sometimes they are louder and darker messages. (*Stop eating and you'll be skinny; cut yourself; kill yourself; it will be easier for everyone if you just died.*)

Here is the truth: God can help you silence the negative voices in your mind. You really can experience God's love and power and tell those lying voices inside your head to shut up!

CHAPTER 1

Say Shut Up

X	**My good friend Mike once said to me, "Christy, everyone has at least one lie they believe about themselves." I agree with Mike. Negative thoughts are like annoying little bees, buzzing around inside our brains, trying to fill our minds with worries. Day after day, these negative thoughts can become so overwhelming that we begin to feel like these feelings are facts. These lies can seem like they are the real truth. When those tormenting thoughts go on for a while, it's not uncommon for teens and young adults to become sad, anxious, depressed, or hopeless. When that happens, people are vulnerable to the Enemy's lies, and when that goes on for a long time, they can have thoughts of harming themselves or even ending their lives.**

Most people (young and old) have a hard time figuring out the different thoughts in their head. We can get confused wondering, *Which thoughts are my own feelings? Which are negative messages from other people? Which voices are dark and dangerous? What is the loving voice of God and how can I hear His voice more?* Sometimes, it's hard to tell, right?

Let me ask you an important question: Do you know what the voice of God sounds like? Do you understand when thoughts inside your mind are negative messages that are tearing you down? Do you know when the thoughts in your mind are actually lies from the Enemy? God wants to show you what messages are good voices and what messages are tearing you down. It's very important for you to know how to identify the different thoughts going on inside your head. You have power when you understand which messages are from God, which are from your own pain, and which are from the Enemy. Once you clearly see and understand these voices, you have even more power to shut them up.

ANNIE'S DREAM

The night Walker jumped in front of that train, my daughter Annie (who was 11 at the time) had a dream. Annie didn't know Walker, and as we tucked her into bed that night, none of us knew yet about this awful thing that had happened. At midnight, the phone rang and our friend told us while sobbing that Walker had committed suicide. My husband, Ben, rushed over to the Eberwein's house to be with their family who were shocked and devastated by this horrible tragedy. The next morning, we had to wake up our girls and tell them the news about Walker because they went to the same school. We knew they would hear kids talking and we wanted them to hear it from us first. With tears in our eyes, we told them that Walker had ended his life. Annie's beautiful brown eyes got very big, and then she burst into tears, and said,

"Mom and Dad, I had this dream last night and I think it was about Walker." Annie has a prophetic gift and often hears God in dreams. She began to tell us the details of her dream: "There were fire trucks and ambulances around train tracks. Jesus came to the ambulance, and when He arrived, something dark flew away. Jesus called angels and told them to take the ambulance up to heaven. Then, Jesus walked over to the dad, and put his arms around him and said,

"Life will come out of death."

Annie didn't know Walker. In fact, she had gone to sleep that night completely unaware that this horrible tragic suicide had happened just 15 minutes away on train tracks nearby. We believe God gave Annie that dream to breathe encouragement into his family that heaven is real, and that the Spirit of God is really with them. It was very comforting to Walker's family that God would give an 11-year-old girl, who didn't even know their son, that powerful dream on the very night he died.

Walker's suicide was like a bomb going off at the school. Kids arrived at school teary-eyed, scared, and shocked at this tragic event. It rocked their sense of security, safety, and their faith. For months to come, students began sharing their own pain. Some confessed to cutting. Others talked about feeling bullied and depressed. Some talked about having experienced abuse. Several kids were brave enough to talk about their own suicidal thoughts.

One day, I asked my high school daughter, Corey, and my middle school daughter, Annie, about what they were seeing among their teenage friends. I was shocked at what they reported to me. The girls told me bluntly,

"Mom, people our age are hurting and feel alone. Sometimes they feel bullied but don't tell their parents or teachers. Some friends will come to us and privately whisper that they are depressed, cutting, or throwing up when no one sees. Even some are threatening to take their own lives. But they don't tell adults."

I trust my girls, so I began to do some research of my own to understand just how widespread the problems are among their generation. I'm thankful to have some friends who are psychologists and doctors that provided me with some of the following data.

If you're like my kids, you are probably sick of research and statistics. In fact, you probably know all about the high suicide rate among your generation and also how many students are anxious, depressed, or facing big problems but telling no one. Here is what I've found myself which I thought might help you or a friend you know not feel so alone, because many, many students your age are in pain, even if they're pretending to be OK in front of their friends.

The following are some of the most recent statistics published by some really well respected research bodies. NIMH says this: "In 2014, 11.4 percent of youths aged 12 to 17 (2.8 million adolescents) had a major depressive episode (MDE) in the past year." [11]

In 2011, the American College Health Association–National College Health Assessment (ACHA–NCHA) compiled data from a nation-wide survey of college students at two-and four-year institutions that found about 30 percent of college students reported feeling "so depressed that it was difficult to function" at some time in the past year. [12]

Depression can also affect your academic performance in college. There is research that says, "College students with depression are twice as likely as their classmates to drop out of school." [13]

In the fall 2011 ACHA–NCHA survey, more than 6 percent of college students reported seriously considering suicide, and about 1 percent reported attempting suicide in the previous year. [14] Suicide is the second leading cause of death for teens and young adults ages 15 to 24. Students should also be aware that the warning signs could be different in men versus in women.

SO WHAT DOES ALL THIS MEAN?

When I talk to large groups of teens or college students, I'll often ask them, "Do those statistics surprise you?" Usually, they tell me something like this,

"Actually, Christy, we are surprised that the statistics aren't higher. We pretty much know this stuff and think those stats are kind of low."

And they're right. Most doctors and therapists will tell you that even though the NIMH and the CDC, for example, publish statistics that have been carefully researched, the numbers are low. That's because they only represent the kids who are actually reporting their problems. And we know that many teens and college students don't want to tell parents, therapists, or teachers that they are suffering. Instead, they suffer alone. Sadly, I think we can safely say that these statistics (which are shocking anyway) are low and more young people are suffering today than is being reported.

If you are a young person reading this book, I want to let you know that for reasons we don't completely understand, many professional doctors and therapists (regardless of their religious beliefs) believe that your generation seems to be under more attack – I think spiritual attack – than ever before. In your generation, we've found over 85 percent believe in forces of good and evil in the world, and feel your generation is under spiritual attack as well. (Check out the next chapter for our *shut up* ministry survey data.)

Is that too dramatic? I don't think so. The statistics above are just the tip of the iceberg when it comes to all the problems facing your generation.

This summer, I've been taking kids out to coffee for their favorite drinks and listening to their ideas. I tell them that when I was in high school, I never even heard of one person committing suicide. No one knew about stuff like cutting. I get angry when some adults minimize the pain facing you guys and respond with, *This kind of stuff has always been going on. We just hear more about it now.* I honestly want to shout SHUT UP right in their faces (but restrain myself, usually). But seriously – that's a really dumb thing to say. It's ignorant and utterly out of touch with how very scary and traumatic life is for young people. Today, it's "normal" now to know friends who are anxious, depressed, doing drugs, throwing up, cutting, or suicidal. It's a very scary time to be a teenager. *But here's the thing: I am convinced that your generation knows way more than most adults, parents, therapists, doctors, and youth pastors about the problems and how to help.* We are all trying our best to help. And yet, there are very real reasons why teens and college students don't feel safe talking to adults when they are hurting.

If you are a young person reading this book, we are praying that this book might help you and your friends. You will hear me say "we" often, because many of the ideas that are in this book are coming from people your age. At the end of every chapter, we've included some questions we hope will help you think about your own life. (BTW: You can reflect on these questions privately or use them in a small group with friends. There are no "right" answers; just share your opinions.) Later, we will connect you with some websites and safe individuals who care and can help you confidentially. We won't pretend to have all the answers, but we believe the Spirit of God is calling us to listen to you. We care that you and your friends are hurting and we want to help you. The next chapter is all about *hearing you*. Your ideas and feedback might even save someone's life.

WHAT DO YOU THINK?

x   Do you know friends who are suffering from anxiety, depression, or are hurting right now?

x   Do you think people in your generation feel safe talking to other adults? Why or why not?

x   If you're facing a problem, who are you most likely to tell?

CHAPTER 2

Your Voice Needs to Be Heard

X   A few years ago, I traveled with 159 middle school students to the East Coast. We had a blast! One day, our three tour busses pulled up in downtown New York City and all 159 middle school students (plus parents and teachers) descended into Times Square. We walked off the busses into a sea of thousands of people and crowded into the streets. It was so loud you could barely hear the person next to you. We were bombarded with videos of fashion models on big screens flashing high above on the tall skyscraper buildings. I walked next to a man dressed up like Buzz Light Year in Toy Story on the other side of the street was a lady who had painted her body completely green and was wearing a

Statue of Liberty costume. Men, women, and children were shoulder-to-shoulder in the streets, pushing and shouting. Many of our students lost their voices that night after screaming over the deafening noises of downtown New York City.

Losing your voice after screaming to be heard in Times Square is understandable. ***It's not OK, though, for you to lose your voice to speak up when you're hurting.*** When you're alone and hurting, and feel you can't tell anyone, it's a horrible feeling. You can feel sad, scared, and lonely.

The immense pressure on teens and college students today is suffocating. My oldest daughter, Corey, is a sophomore in high school. Last year, she ran a fever for over a year with extreme abdominal pain and despite countless blood tests, doctor visits, ultrasounds, and MRIs, no one could figure out why Corey was so sick. One night, the pain was so bad that we ended up in Urgent Care and they finally found a tumor (the size of a tennis ball) on her ovary. She ended up at Lucille Packard hospital and we heard some doctors in the hallway whispering about ovarian cancer. It was a scary time. Our good friend Dr. Christie Coleman is a surgeon and rushed to the hospital. The next day, Christie did Corey's surgery and removed this large tumor, which was thankfully a big cyst and not cancerous. We are forever thankful to Jesus, our praying friends, and doctors who helped us through it.

Corey is better now, but it's been a long, hard journey over the past year. She missed much of her freshman and sophomore year. Thanks to The King's Academy staff and students, she's been able to catch up. She's lucky because she's strong academically, but it's been very stressful.

No matter what school you attend, the academic pressure these days is crazy. If you play sports, or do theatre, or whatever else after school, you probably have even more pressure to perform and then end up with hours of homework every night. Not only that, you guys have to deal with stuff like cyber bullying and the drama of being a teen or college student today. People in authority (principals, teachers, coaches, parents) need to seriously look at the pressure that society today is putting on you. We need to understand that this stress you're carrying is one of the factors contributing to insomnia, depression, anxiety, eating disorders, other mental illnesses, and more serious issues like cutting and suicide among teens today.

Sleep deprivation is a common problem among most teens and college students and is a huge contributing factor to making your generation tired, depressed, anxious, and even suicidal. Your parents might not understand this, but you do. Because of the high pressure to perform, many of you are staying up late into the night and then have to wake up early for school, only to repeat this pattern day after day.

An article published by the *Stanford Medicine Magazine* has this to say about sleep deprivation:

> *According to a 2006 National Sleep Foundation poll, the organization's most recent survey of teen sleep, more than 87 percent of high school students in the United States get far less than the recommended eight to 10 hours, and the amount of time they sleep is decreasing — a serious threat to their health, safety, and academic success. Sleep deprivation increases the likelihood teens will suffer myriad negative consequences, including an inability to concentrate, poor grades, drowsy-driving incidents, anxiety, depression, thoughts of suicide and even suicide attempts. It's a problem that knows no economic boundaries.*

> *While studies show that both adults and teens in industrialized nations are becoming more sleep deprived, the problem is most acute among teens, said Nanci Yuan, MD, director of the Stanford Children's Health Sleep Center. In a detailed 2014 report, the American Academy of Pediatrics called the problem of tired teens a public health epidemic.*

> *"I think high school is the real danger spot in terms of sleep deprivation," said William Dement, MD, Ph.D., founder of the Stanford Sleep Disorders Clinic, the first of its kind in the world.*

"It's a huge problem. What it means is that nobody performs at the level they could perform," whether it's in school, on the roadways, on the sports field or in terms of physical and emotional health. [15]

As I talk to teens and college students today, they will confidentially tell me that they don't feel like people are listening to them. Many of them will say something like,

"Christy, I feel like I have no voice to speak up when I'm hurting. I think the adults around me will just think I'm being dramatic and exaggerating." I know that many of you feel unheard and believe that your voice just doesn't matter above the expectations of parents, grades, clubs, and colleges. If that's you, I want to say something very important to you: ***Your voice needs to be heard!*** You deserve a place to have your voice heard above all the other deafening voices of school and work and clubs. You deserve to have safe people listen to you.

Since March of 2014, we have been interviewing teens and college students about their experiences with social media, academic pressure, friendships, depression, anxiety, eating disorders, cutting, and suicide. In March of 2014, 2015, and 2016, we have spoken to over a thousand students at conferences, middle and high schools, and colleges. We have given them handouts and invited them to fill out our *shut up* survey to give us their ideas. We spent hours talking to them and getting their honest, unedited feedback.

From the written surveys and www.sayshutup.com surveys, we have received over 350 answers. Check out the questions and responses.

SHUT UP SURVEY RESULTS

If you are hurting (depressed, anxious, suicidal, or have another painful problem) are you most likely to tell (a) parents (b) teacher (c) counselor (d) youth pastor (e) friend.

70% A friend
10% Parents
10% No one
5% A favorite teacher or youth pastor
5% Counselor

Do you know of someone who has committed suicide or who is suicidal right now?

85% Yes
10% Don't know
5% No

When a friend tells you they are hurting themselves or suicidal, what do you do?

85% I don't tell an adult because my friend asked me not to, but then I'm worried he or she will do it and I'll be responsible.

10% I tell my parents and take the risk he or she will be mad at me.

5% I go tell a teacher.

What are the main reasons that you (or your friends) won't tell an adult if you're struggling with depression, painful thoughts, anxiety, or suicidal thoughts? (The most commonly listed reasons appear below.)

1. I'm ashamed.

2. I don't think an adult will really believe me and will just say I'm being hormonal, moody, or over dramatic.

3. I'm afraid I'll be judged.

4. I don't think anyone can really help me.

5. I have a fear of being punished if I say something.

6. I feel like my parents (or other adults) are part of the problem, and they'll just blame it on me and that will make me feel even worse.

7. I'm afraid they'll make me go to a counselor and that won't help.

How many hours of sleep are you getting at night?

5%   9 hours

10%   7 hours

85%   6 hours or less

If you're hurting, would you be willing to see a counselor? Why or why not?

83%   No*

Comments from this group included being "afraid of being judged," and "it wouldn't be a safe place to open up." Most said they "didn't think it would help."

17% Maybe*

> This group was indecisive. Responders indicated they might see a counselor but would have to trust him or her and were simultaneously afraid of being labeled or judged.

NOTE: We will tell you more about how good counselors can help but the problem of actually finding these people and how to go about it is in chapter nine, "Find Safe People (Who Will Shut Up and Listen)."

What are the things that are causing you the most pressure in your life?

- Academics
- Sports
- Peer Pressure
- Bullying
- Feeling alone in my pain
- Bad self-esteem or not liking how I look
- Relationship break-ups
- Pressure to do drugs
- Pressure to drink
- Fear of STDs
- Not feeling good enough
- Fear of punishment over not good enough grades
- Pressure to get into college

College students added these to the list:
- Financial pressure and fear about paying student loans
- Fear of never finding someone to marry
- Pressure to drink, do drugs, sleep around, and have unsafe sex
- Fear of not being successful in life

Do you believe in God?

90% Yes
7% Maybe
3% No

Do you believe in demons?

70% Yes
18% Maybe
12% No

Do you think social media is part of the reason teens and college students are more depressed, anxious, or suicidal today?

50% Yes
50% No

My kids warned me that I should *not* do a chapter on social media. For one thing, I'm a social media idiot. Annie says I'm one of those moms who tries to zoom in on Instagram pictures and ends up liking them on accident. So, I'm not kidding when I say I don't have a clue about social media. I also understand that many of you have very different feelings, positive and negative, when it comes to social media. Still, we all felt I should at least comment on social media, and the impact it might have on the problems teens and college students have today, because it's such an important part of your world.

As you can see from the 50/50 split above, teens and college students we surveyed are very divided on this issue. Big picture: Most teens and college students said that social media can be a good thing, or a destructive thing, depending on how it's used. For example, you've probably heard stories about people who have been really hurt by cyber bullying. One teen at our school was threatened (anonymously) by another student until the threats got so severe that they even claimed that they were going to kill her. Consequently, this girl was so afraid to come to school and became severely anxious and depressed. No one ever figured out who it was despite all the searching by police and staff, and it eventually stopped.

You've all probably heard stories or seen reports on the news about people who have sent nude selfies (or others have done it) and then these photos were spread to others, resulting in depression and even suicide. Here is one example of how using social media in a destructive way took someone's life. Check out one girl's story:

> She's a 15-year-old girl in Florida known for laughing, cheer leading and flag football. Some friends of hers allegedly took nude photos of her and spread them to their groups of friends without her consent. The bullying got so bad that Tovanna couldn't handle it anymore. She took the handgun out of her mother's purse and shot herself in her bathroom.
>
> I don't get it. I know Tovanna isn't alone. 160,000 kids per day skip school out of fear of being bullied.
>
> I get social media is fun, I get everyone's on there, I get that you live in a world that maybe hasn't totally been introduced to consequences, but we need to learn from the consequences of this story. We need to learn that society is turning full speed toward disaster and we have two choices, stay on the bus or stand up and fight against evils like this. Don't take naked pictures. Not of yourself, not of others. Even if someone asks you to, it's your opportunity to talk to them about the true meaning of beauty. If a guy is going to leave you if you don't send him nudes then that's the perfect sign to break up with him. I promise. [16]

That number above (160,000 kids per day skip school) may not be an accurate number. It's probably higher. Recent research from the CDC on bullying will be discussed in chapter five with ideas for you about what to do if you or someone you know is being bullied.

This past spring, Annie suffered a concussion and had terrible headaches for two months. Unfortunately, she had to miss a lot of school and also graduation parties at the end of the year. Annie loves being with her friends and it was depressing to be isolated at home, missing school, and fun parties. One night, she was home with a bad headache and noticed that her friends were posting pictures of a party. I felt really sad for Annie and we tried to have a fun family movie night because we knew she was feeling lonely.

At the same time, many teens and college students will quickly point out all the positive things social media is doing that helps your generation. Social media can keep you connected to your friends who are often your biggest encouragers, and you can feel less lonely when you're talking to your friends online. Social media can also connect you to help when you need it. Without social media, we couldn't even have our website or ministry, which will connect you to other books, resources, counselors, pastors, or friends who can help you. Bottom line: The 50/50 split regarding social media is probably a good representation of your generation's overall feelings. The take-away? Use social media wisely. Enjoy your friends and stay connected to positive sites and people. Think twice before sending nudes or other things that can go viral and come back to hurt you or someone else. Don't use social media to bully other people. When I worked in Washington, D.C., we had a saying: Don't put anything in writing you don't want to be seen on the news the next day. The same thing applies to social media. Don't put anything on social media that you wouldn't want your friends, parents, or teachers to see.

So, cool story. Last summer, I flew to Jacksonville, Florida to visit my family. On the long flight from San Francisco to Jacksonville, I worked on my laptop writing this book. My son, Benji, was giving me his ideas and we worked on the book together on the flight across the country. The plane landed and as we were gathering our backpacks and bags from under the seat, God spoke to me through a teenage angel: A young girl who was sitting behind me on the plane looked at me and said in a sweet voice,

"On the flight, I was looking over your shoulder as you wrote on your laptop. I just want you to know it's going to be a really good book and it will help a lot of people."

Was she a real angel? Not really. But I believe God sent her to me with this encouraging message at a time when I wanted to give up writing. This young person was kind enough to email me later and tell me her name, Kaitlyn. I'm thankful to Kaitlyn and the hundreds of young people who have taken time to share their stories and ideas with me. Without their help, I would never have finished this book and I feel thankful to have written this book with such wise teens and college students. Their ideas are awesome and their stories inspire me.

What do you think? If you would be willing to take a few minutes to share your opinions of what you think, I would be very grateful. If you have a story, or ideas about how to help people who are hurting in your generation, I would love to know what you think. You can email me at: christy@sayshutup.com.

Lastly, if you are someone who values people being real and honest about their pain, I think the next chapter will encourage you. It can be very lonely to suffer privately and feel like no one understands what you're going through. Five young friends gave me permission to tell you their stories. They are courageous young people who were willing to risk being vulnerable with their own stories, because they want you to know that, despite painful chapters in life, it's possible to go on and find healing and hope.

WHAT DO YOU THINK?

x   Why do teens and college students believe they don't have a voice?

x   How many hours of sleep are you getting each night? How does lack of sleep affect your mood and life?

x   What are the top three things in your life that are causing you to be stressed?

x   If you were hurting, who are you most likely to tell?

CHAPTER 3

It Takes Guts to Tell Your Story (Julie, Devon, Justin, Carrie, and Kimm Speak Out)

X   It takes guts to share your story. That's especially true if you have painful chapters in your life. I'm very thankful to have five young friends who have courageously shared their stories for this book. As you listen to their stories, I believe you will be encouraged that no matter how big your problems might feel right now, there is always hope.

The following are real stories shared by teenagers and college students. With the exception of Julie, the names and some details have been changed to protect their identities.

Julie
Perfectionist at school. Played college volleyball. Went to New York City to model. Life seemed perfect on the surface, but she almost took her own life.

My name is Julie and I have been happily married to the most amazing man for 10 years. We have two beautiful little girls. I am so blessed and grateful for my life; however, it wasn't always like this. At one time I thought I could never be used by God in my brokenness and never knew the power I had in Jesus to say *shut up* to the negative thoughts in my mind.

As a child, I was very driven and ambitious, competitive, and wanted to be the best at everything. I looked for love and affirmation in all the wrong places. Addicted to achievements and success, I accomplished a lot at a young age and everyone probably thought I was happy. I was good at pretending everything was fine even when I was hurting on the inside. I was a straight-A student, leader of many groups, an all-around athlete, high school valedictorian, went on to become a runway and print model in Chicago and New York and received a full-ride Division I college volleyball scholarship.

Many of these accomplishments were about me trying to earn people's love. It never worked because I was riddled with anxiety on the inside. Secretly, I was battling low self-esteem, self-hatred, depression, performance anxiety, perfectionism, suicidal thoughts, guilt, and shame. Because of the stress and pressure, I had chronic migraines.

I hated myself and was terrified people would find out who I really was which made me feel like a phony. Not even my best friends knew how much I was hurting. As a result, I suffered alone and my depression and anxiety went untreated for years. Often, I thought about ending my life. Suicidal thoughts got worse and worse. Secretly, I would act out sexually, getting drunk, and doing other very self-destructive things to try to numb the pain. It was a vicious cycle. I would be good and happy until something didn't go right or a break-up happened with a guy and I would spiral back into a very dark suicidal place again.

I believed in God and was crying out for help every day. But I felt so much shame for my thoughts that it was hard for me to experience God's presence and grace. Instead I believed so many lies from the Enemy, and looking back I know he was trying to destroy me by the constant voices telling me it would be better if I died. The Bible says in 1 Peter 5:8, "Your Enemy the devil prowls around like a roaring lion looking for someone to devour" (NIV). That was happening to me and I began to feel so miserable that I believed the Enemy's lie that it would be better to die than endure the pain.

On the night of March 19, 2005 at the age of 23, I attempted suicide at my ex-boyfriend's apartment by downing as many pills as I could find with a huge bottle of alcohol. (Thankfully, there weren't too many options in the place, otherwise it could have been way worse.) We had been madly in love, and I really did feel like this was the guy that God wanted me to marry, but hidden sin in our relationship began to poison us and ended up breaking us apart. I felt so much shame. The breakup felt like God was punishing me for all my mistakes in the relationship – that was why I couldn't have what I wanted. The night we broke up, I felt a complete loss of control over my pain, an all-encompassing self-hatred, and the rejection and abandonment became too much to bear. When you put a relationship up so high above God it feels like a death when it's over. I couldn't stand up against the weight of the pain anymore. I remember when I was swallowing the pills, I even said aloud,

"I can't believe I'm doing this." But then, I heard a dark, oppressive voice whisper back, *But you must do it. It's the only way out.* So much of what I heard and felt in that moment was oppressive and heavy – the pain was never going to end, and I was never going to be good enough to be loved. Even though I was a Christian, all I heard that dark night was the lie over and over again: *God doesn't love you*.

Looking back, I know I really didn't want to die that night, but I just wanted the pain to go away as fast as possible and was completely hopeless and humiliated for the way that I handled the break-up. Some of his friends had even called me a "crazy ex-girlfriend," which I honestly never thought I would be called in my life, considering I had always been a people pleaser and wanted everyone to not only like me but *love* all of me. I just wanted to run away, and since I believed in Jesus I thought heaven sounded way better than earth. Thankfully, my ex-boyfriend knew I was not in a good state of mind the night he left so he called one of my good friends and prayer partners from church to come check on me. She called and called but got no answer. Worried, she came over and arrived as I was going in and out of consciousness. She called the paramedics in time to rush me to the hospital to the emergency room to pump my stomach of the poison. It was brutal and painful, and when I came back to myself that next morning, all I felt at first was more shame and embarrassment. Then, inexplicably, I had this weird peace that came over me slowly throughout the day, and I felt so relieved and free that I didn't have to hide anymore; my pain was now out in the open. The world could see the depth of my sadness. I felt God's presence and sensed that one day He would use this pain for good. From the days that followed, I began to see life differently. I was grateful for who God had created me to be. I no longer wanted to die when circumstances seemed hopeless, and I understood pain was temporary, but more than that, I could turn to Jesus to comfort me no matter how deep the sadness was.

God saved my life. I'm forever grateful that God intervened and that I'm still alive today. He transformed my life through the power of the Holy Spirit. Looking back, I now understand that I did not really want to die that day, I just wanted the pain to go away. It's scary to think that if I had been successful in my suicide attempt, I would have missed out on this amazing life God has given me: my husband, my daughters, and now a ministry encouraging young people that they can hear God's loving voice which can heal them and with God's help, they can shut up the Enemy's lies. I still battle depression and anxiety from time to time, but I don't go to that terrible place of wanting to die. I don't turn to destructive things or stay in hiding, but I turn to God, His Word, prayer, and safe friends who want to encourage me with the truth.

I want you all to find the same joy and hope I did in Jesus and to have the courage to find a safe place and friends to share your inner struggles to gain the power back from the Enemy who wants you to feel like you are alone. I pray that you would know your true value and identity in Christ and that you are loved just the way you are. I would love to hear your story and pray for you if you want to connect with me. Just email me at info@sayshutup.com.

Christy here. Julie is now one of my very best friends and my partner in ministry. If you want to hear more about Julie's story, you can see the video of her testimony on my website at www.christypierce.org. She is a compassionate prayer warrior who is now helping hundreds of young people.

Devon

Bullied at middle school. Became depressed and addicted to porn. Made a plan to end his life.

I grew up in a Christian family. In middle school, I wasn't really one of the popular kids, and if you've ever watched The Middle, I was a little like Brick (the nice but nerdy kind of kid who liked to be alone). I didn't have a lot of friends. One day as I was walking home from school, three other boys who were big football players, the popular guys, started by calling me names: "Hey nerd boy, don't you have anything better to do than read those stupid books?" or "Are you gay?" or "Why don't you man up and play sports like us?"

Even though their words hurt, I pretended I didn't hear them. I walked faster and faster, almost running home, and then hid in my room and cried. The next day, they followed me from school again, but this time the bullying got worse. I kept my head down trying to ignore their laughing behind me, but then they pushed me into the school fence and laughed as I dropped all my books. I was afraid to tell my parents or teachers because I thought the bullying might get worse. Every morning, I was scared to go to school, and I started getting stomachaches every morning. I begged my parents to stay home from school. Eventually, they took me to the doctor, and after awhile, my doctor said it would be good to return to school. No one knew the real reason that I wanted to stay home. I knew my parents were worried about me and they cared, but I didn't feel safe telling them because I was so afraid they would tell the principal and these guys would be even madder at me. I didn't want to be labeled a snitch and I kept having pictures in my head of these bullies beating me up. So, I stayed quiet. A year later, I went to high school. The bullying stopped, but their voices were stuck inside my head and I started to believe they were right, and I kept hearing their words inside my head: *I'm a nerd. I'm a loser and weak. I'll never be successful in life.*

That year, I started to get very depressed. I didn't want to get out of bed. I was sad and weepy (when no one could see me). One night, I got on the Internet, and I saw porn for the first time. At first, it made me feel good to look at these porn sites and it distracted me from these inner-tormenting thoughts. I even thought to myself, *Those guys might think I'm cool now because I'm sneaking around at night to look at porn.*

But the more I looked, the more addicted I became to porn, and then I started to hate myself. These negative, cruel, self-loathing kinds of messages started becoming so loud in my head one day that I didn't want to live anymore. I kept thinking to myself, *Things are hopeless. I hate myself. No one sees me. This pain will go on for the rest of my life and I can't take it anymore.* That's when I made a plan to end my life. Since I lived near the train tracks, I planned to sneak out at night and jump in front of the train. That night, I took a shower and an amazing thing happened. I was thinking about this plan to jump in front of the train, and I heard a loud voice say to me, *Devon I love you. You are not alone and I can stop this pain. For I know the plans I have for you, says the Lord, plans to prosper you and give you a future and a hope.*

I began crying uncontrollably, and as the water poured over me, I felt this incredible peace like I had never known before. I felt loved and for the first time in my life, I felt safe. The next day, a friend I barely knew, invited me to a church youth group. The youth pastors were really nice, and one of them came and asked if he could take me for coffee after school the next day. That was a new beginning for me. I really believe that God saved my life. Instead of listening to those shaming voices that had been tearing me down for years, I began to hear the loving voice of God through my pastors and new friends. The porn? Well, I just stopped. One day I prayed and asked God to help me stop, and He must have given me power because somehow I didn't have a desire to do it anymore. I felt accepted, loved, and not alone for the first time in my life.

Carrie
Depressed after being molested by her gymnastics coach.

I loved gymnastics from the time I was three years old. When I started kindergarten, I remember I couldn't wait for the bell to ring, and I would run to the car. My mom would take me to gymnastics and I would get on the balance beam. Being on the balance beam was my happy place. All through junior high and high school, I did competitive gymnastics. Three years in a row, I won at the state tournament. My sophomore year in high school, though, was super hard because my parents got divorced. Honestly, I was pretty devastated by the divorce, and hated all the fighting over me. To escape the yelling and fights, I threw myself even more into gymnastics because it had always been the thing I loved.

My high school gymnastics coach requested more hours with me, asking me to stay late in the evenings to practice. Honestly, I thought that would be better than going home to more arguing. But I was wrong. One night, when no one was at the school, my gymnastics coach began to touch me inappropriately. I knew it was wrong, but I was ashamed and shocked when he was doing it. I was afraid to tell anyone and didn't think they would believe me, so I kept letting him do it and he kept pushing me to do more. One night, I started crying and begged him to stop. He told me that if I told anyone else, he would deny it and no one would believe me.

For three months, I told no one. This lying voice inside my head kept saying, *You are disgusting. You are a whore, and it's probably your fault he started touching you. No one will believe you if you speak up.* Pretty soon, I became so depressed that I didn't want to leave my house. My parents thought I was upset about the divorce (which I was, of course, but the sexual abuse was the worst part). I felt out of control, so I stopped eating and became anorexic.

Six months later, I couldn't take the pain anymore and so I told my mom what happened. Mom was furious at the coach, and he was eventually fired. I had to go to another school, though, and that was very hard. Mom got me lots of help. She found a counselor who was kind, and going to counseling helped, but I was still very sad. So my mom took me to her friend who prays for people (and I thought this was going to be really weird and agreed reluctantly).

Christy opened the door, and I knew that this was going to be a God thing. We started meeting at a coffee shop on Sundays. Christy would pray for me, and God would show her these mental pictures of me, that were crazy because they were so right on! Every Sunday, I looked forward to meeting, because when Christy and I were praying together, that's when I started to hear God's voice through the Holy Spirit. One night, we left the coffee shop with our lattes and climbed into Christy's minivan to pray.

While Christy was praying, all of a sudden, she stopped and said, "Carrie, I see a picture of you in a white dress and I hear the word 'Arwen.' Does that mean anything to you?"

I was blown away. Arwen was my favorite character in *The Lord of The Rings* book and movie. She is a mighty warrior and basically kicks the butts of all the bad guys. I told Christy about my favorite Arwen scene in the movie, when she rescues Frodo by carrying his wounded body on a galloping white horse followed by eight black demonic creatures riding black horses. Arwen crosses the river and shouts,

"If you want him, come and get him!" The black horses start to attack Arwen and she calls down spiritual power that wipes the black horses and demonic riders away.

That prayer time was a turning point for me. There was no way that Christy could have known that Arwen was my hero, but God did. Seeing myself through God's eyes, as a mighty warrior like Arwen, was so healing and freeing. I didn't feel damaged, dirty, or hopeless anymore. Now, I'm studying to be a pastor. I want to be a warrior for God, and help other girls who have been abused find hope and healing through God's love.

Justin
Pressure from varsity soccer pushed him to post nudes, do drugs, and eventually attempt suicide.

I started playing soccer when I was five years old. My dad was a big soccer player in high school and always dreamed he could play in college, but he had a bad knee injury his senior year in high school and he never had the chance to play in college. All through elementary school, I played soccer and everyone said I was really good. The club teams recruited me and soccer became my life, because I practiced at least two hours a day, and joined the traveling soccer team when I started middle school. After two years with the traveling soccer team, I wanted to quit. Even though I was one of the star players, I realized one day that soccer was no longer fun for me. Part of the problem was that I felt pressure everywhere I turned. My dad and coach were constantly pushing me to do better in soccer. When I got home late at night, I was exhausted and just wanted to sleep, but would stay up late at night to finish algebra and my other homework. Sports were easy for me, but school was hard. My teachers started pressuring me to do better in school and no matter how hard I tried, I couldn't do better. One day, I told my parents that I wanted to quit soccer and my dad blew up. He was screaming and had a red face, saying that I would never get into a good college unless I got a soccer scholarship and that he wasn't going to pay for college.

To make my dad happy, I kept playing soccer. Secretly, I began to hate soccer. It was my dad's dream, but it wasn't my dream. I made the varsity team. My parents never knew that I was miserable at school and was afraid that I would fail my classes. I was feeling so afraid all the time that I started having panic attacks. (I didn't know what they were then, but now I do.) It was scary. My heart would be racing, and I couldn't breathe. Then, I developed insomnia. I had trouble falling asleep and when I did, I would wake up terrified in the night. About this time, I began hanging out with a crowd of kids who were into drugs and partying. Looking back, I think I was looking for some way to numb my pain and escape.

At night, we would go to parties and everyone was smoking pot and having sex. That's when I met Veronica. She was pretty and the first girl that I thought finally understood me. I even told her about hating soccer and how afraid I was that I might fail at school. My panic attacks went away because I was finally telling someone about my problems and I didn't feel so alone. One night, some guys were pressuring me to post nude pictures of myself and send them to Veronica. I was drunk, so I did it. The next day, I woke up and realized what I had done and felt so ashamed I wanted to die. I had hoped that Veronica hadn't gotten the pictures, but that afternoon, Veronica texted me and told me she had met a new football player that she wanted to date instead of me. Just like that. She broke up with me through a text. That night, I went out and smoked pot with those guys, and one guy offered me cocaine, so I just left the party. Somehow I made it home that night, but when I got home, my dad was awake. He smelled the pot and started yelling at me, saying I would never be successful in life because I was throwing my life away using drugs and girls.

That night, I crawled into bed and cried myself to sleep. No one knew how hopeless I felt and that I didn't want to live anymore. No one knew I was suicidal. Every day, I would show up at soccer practice and school. Now I can see that I was in a private hell of my own pain and I remember thinking, *The pain will never stop. No one will even miss me when I'm gone. At least I can finally stop playing soccer.* So, I formed a plan in my mind to end my life. My dad is a hunter so he kept guns in our garage. One night I waited until everyone else was asleep. After midnight, I snuck into the garage and found my dad's loaded shotgun. I was planning to put that gun in my mouth and pull the trigger, but that's when I saw something that saved my life.

The only way to describe it was that a gold, warm light filled the whole garage and I felt this strange calm peace come over me and I heard a voice say to me, *Justin, I love you and I have a plan for your life that is good. You can't see it now, but trust Me, and I will show you the way out.* You have to understand that I had never been to church before and we weren't a religious family at all. Still, I knew that this voice was really God and that I was going to be OK somehow. So, I carefully put the gun back, and went up to my room and fell asleep. That night, for the first time in a long time, I slept peacefully and woke up feeling like a dark cloud had lifted from my life.

For the first time in years, I was no longer afraid. I ditched my old friends and decided I needed to find a church. A girl at school told me about her youth group, so I just showed up one day. Some guys were in a small group and they invited me to join. These guys share the real unedited stuff going on and don't try to hide things from each other. We don't judge each other. We listen and then we pray. Through these friends, I finally got up the guts to quit soccer. My dad was pissed at first, but now he is supporting me. I'm planning to be a P.E. teacher and really excited about helping students because it's tough these days to grow up in our world.

Kimm
Hospitalized during high school after an eating disorder became an emergency.

I'm a senior in high school and thankful to be out of the hospital. My story is sad but I hope it will help someone so I'm mustering up the courage to tell it. My parents immigrated from China 20 years ago and they are extremely hard working. My dad earned a medical degree from Boston University and went on to become one of the leading heart surgeons on the West Coast. Both my parents feel strongly that academic excellence is mandatory for all of us kids. I'm proud of my parents, and I understand that they really only want us to be successful in life, but I really don't think they have any idea how much pressure they put on us. Once I got a B+ and my parents were so angry that they threatened to give my dog away if I did it again. It broke my heart and even though I'm a Christian, it's very hard to forgive them. All throughout high school, I was filled with fear about making good grades. Everyone at school called me the "smart girl" but I'm really not that smart. I just stayed up every night until midnight and studied. I was terrified of failure and constantly worried that I would never live up to my parent's expectations.

Because my mom grew up in very poor family in China, there was never enough food to eat. Every night, we are expected to eat everything on our plate. During freshman year, I started a bad habit and it got worse with time. Because I wanted to get studying, I would eat quickly but after dinner, I would sneak upstairs into my bathroom and secretly vomit. For years I did this, and then my doctor noticed how much weight I had lost, and eventually my bulimia was discovered. My parents were furious and I thought they might disown me. They told me that they didn't understand how I could do something so shameful in the family given all the blessings they had given me. I became even more depressed, and the eating disorder got worse. Eventually, I lost so much weight, that the doctor said I needed to be hospitalized. It was nearly impossible to keep up the rigorous academic schedule, so I had to drop out of school for the last semester of my sophomore year. Thankfully, the hospital staff understood my illness and assigned me a very kind counselor. (I knew she really got it because she had an eating disorder too when she was in college.) My parents really do love me, and even though they didn't understand, they tried to support me and met with the doctors. They also found a pastor who came to visit me and pray for me. My counselor and pastor loved me and helped me. They also somehow got through to my parents that while it's good to have your children be successful in life, too much pressure can make your children sick. Through these people supporting us, things got much better. I was able to do summer school and go back full-time junior year. I won't pretend that things are perfect now, but I'm learning how to love myself and accept God's unconditional love. I'm not perfect, but I've come to realize that it's very freeing to know that God loves me just as I am, not because of what I do.

WHAT'S YOUR STORY?

Julie, Devon, Carrie, Justin, and Kimm are amazing young people that I'm proud to call my friends. Each of them are very humble people who would be the first to tell you that they aren't perfect and still have some hard days. If you could talk to them personally, they each would tell you that they started to find healing when they had real-life encounters with God.

When the Spirit of God spoke to them in different ways, they felt un-conditionally loved and safe. They are also big fans of this *shut up* book and ministry, because they each felt that an important part of their healing journey happened when they stopped believing the negative voices tearing them down, and started to see themselves through God's loving eyes.

What is your story? If you could talk with my young friends, there is one thing I know for sure they would say: Don't stay alone in your pain. You can pray right now and ask God for help. Justin says to tell you that if you don't feel comfortable praying, that's awesome because prayer is just talking to God. Carrie wrote a simple prayer below that she used to pray in her bed each night when she felt alone and depressed. There are some practical things you can do for your-self that will help you shut up the negative voices that are tormenting you. There really are some safe people out there that you can trust who can help. How do you do that? How can you find those people? In chapter eight, we are going to show you some ways you can shut up those negative voices in your head. We believe God is going to help you turn down the volume on the voices tearing you down and turn up the volume on the kind, loving voice of God.

You have your own unique life journey. I'm guessing that there are some happy chapters and some painful chapters. You may be in a painful chapter right now as you're reading this book. Along with my five brave young friends, I want to encourage you to share your story with God and then someone safe that you trust. Sharing your story with safe people can be very healing. Make sure that the people you share your story with commit that it's confidential and that they are encouraging friends. Please don't keep your story hidden. Please don't stay alone.

It can be healing to write down your own story as well. I want to invite you to take some time and write down here (or somewhere else confidential) your own story. What are the good things in your life? What are the hard things? This is a confidential, safe opportunity (just between you and God) to bring "into the light" the things that are heavy and weighing you down. For now, just write them down and notice them. Pay attention to the negative messages that are tearing you down inside (you might not have even recognized them before). It's very important for you to know that the pain you're feeling may seem like it will never end, but it can be stopped. You can feel happy again.

Your voice matters. You deserve to have safe people in your life that will listen to you. God is listening to you right now, even if you feel far away from Him. Whatever you have done, know that God loves you more than you can possibly imagine, and He looks at you with eyes of love, not judgment. God is real and loves you. You are not alone.

Carrie's favorite scene in *The Lord of the Rings* movie when Arwen bravely defeats the evil, dark horses:

Check out YouTube and search for "Arwen rescues Frodo."

One of Justin's prayers he wanted to share with you in case you might want to use it yourself:

"God, it's me, Justin. I'm feeling pretty alone and don't know how to keep going. Please show up for me. Send me a sign that you're here and help me know that you love me and have a plan, even if I can't see it. Amen."

Julie's favorite Bible verse:

"God is close to the broken hearted and He saves those who are crushed in spirit." (Psalm 34:18, NIV)

Devon's favorite song on hard days: "If You Only Knew" by the Sidewalk Prophets:

If you only knew that I am with you every moment
If you only knew that you are never alone
If you only knew the plans that I have for you
And the way that I have told you
Don't you know that you're my own if you only knew
If you only knew
But I already know
Oh, my God I long to know you more and more each day

Kimm's favorite Bible verse she memorized and says to herself when she's afraid:

"Peace I leave with you; my peace I give you. I do not give to you as the world gives. Do not let your hearts be troubled and do not be afraid." (John 14:27, NIV)

YOUR STORY

We've left a blank place here for you to write down your own story.
You may want to keep it confidential between you and God, but if you
want to send it to us, we would love to hear from you. Julie will keep
them confidential and you can email her at info@sayshutup.com.
God can take your painful chapters and make them beautiful.

WHAT DO YOU THINK?

x   Which person's story in this chapter inspired you the most and why?

x   When you're hurting, what things help you make it through each day?

x   It can be healing to share your own story. If you feel comfortable, share your own story with your friends in the group. (P.S.: It's important that the group commits to one another that this is a safe, confidential place to share. It's also OK if you don't want to talk!)

CHAPTER 4

Your Feelings Matter

X   One Saturday night, I went to see, Disney Pixar's *Inside Out*. You may not have seen it, so I'll give you the general idea. The movie is about a little girl, Riley, and the feelings inside her head. Feelings named Joy, Anger, Sadness, Fear, and Disgust were all colorful little characters inside Riley's brain. The dominant feeling in Riley's head was a character named Joy and that feeling dominated Riley's personality. She was happy most of the time, laughing and enjoying her family and friends. Until something hard happened in her life. Then, the other feelings began to take over in Riley's brain. Anger, Fear, and Sadness became the loudest voices. When that happened, Riley became very anxious, angry, and sad. She cried a lot and was scared to go to school. Thankfully, things for Riley turned out OK. Eating popcorn in that dark theater, I thought about many of my teenage friends who have helped me write this book. They have experienced feelings of anger, sadness, and fear, and I'm aware that when those feelings go on a long time (especially if no one helps you understand them), they can become overwhelming. When these thoughts start to take over in your brain, you begin to think your feelings are facts. You can start to think that you will always be angry, afraid, or sad. You begin to lose hope that you can ever be happy again.

Now, it's very important to understand that feelings aren't "bad" in and of themselves. All feelings inside of us can be helpful in various ways. Anger can help you stand up to people and say "no more" when they are hurting you. Fear can help you stay away from things that might be dangerous. What is bad is when certain feelings take over and become the loudest voice inside your head. That's especially true if those voices are only anger, fear, or sadness. Most of us would love to have joy be our dominant feeling, and it can be painful when we get stuck in negative thoughts and feelings. When the loudest voices inside our brain are sadness, anger, fear, depression, anxiety, or hopelessness, life can become very hard and frightening.

UNDERSTANDING DEPRESSION

When I was only five years old, my baby brother, Robbie, died tragically of Sudden Infant Death Syndrome (SIDS). (That's when a baby dies for no explainable reason while asleep.) At that time, a fear of death and deep sadness took over in me and those feelings were buried for a long time. They didn't surface again until middle school when my family moved, and I needed to start a new school. Like Riley in the movie, I missed my old school and friends. Like Riley, I became angry, sad, and cried a lot. I know now what I didn't know then: I was experiencing depression. You can't really fully understand depression unless you've experienced it yourself. Depression can become so overwhelming that you don't want to leave the house, go to school, or do what used to be fun. In extreme cases, depression can make you not want to live anymore. It's very important that you understand the signs of depression, because there is good news: Depression can be healed. There are many things you can do to help yourself when you're depressed and there are things other people can do to help you, if you'll let them.

Maybe you're familiar with depression or know a friend who is going through depression right now. It often helps to understand what's happening inside our minds. When we talk about "shutting up" negative voices, we need to be careful to not shut down the hurting voices that need to be heard.

Sometimes young people feel weak, ashamed, or embarrassed about being depressed. They may even think it's their fault. If that's you, I want you to hear what doctors at the NIMH say about what causes depression:

– *Depression is not your fault or caused by something you did wrong.*

– *Depression is a real, treatable brain illness, or health problem.*

– *Depression can be caused by big transitions in life, stress, or changes in your body's chemicals that affect your thoughts and moods.*

– *Depression can run in families. Maybe you haven't realized that you have depression and have been blaming yourself for being negative.*

– *Remember that depression is not your fault!* [17]

Not only that, if you've ever been depressed, you should know that you are not alone. The number of teens and college students who are depressed today is staggering.

My assistant, Julie (the one who attempted suicide in college and just courageously shared her story in chapter three), was speaking to a large group of college students at the University of California at Los Angeles (UCLA) about depression and anxiety. Afterwards, students lined up to talk with her and have her pray for them. What she heard from these UCLA college students was similar to what the research is telling us about how many college students are suffering from depression and anxiety today.

According to researchers at UCLA, which has been surveying freshman classes for five decades, the emotional health of incoming students has been declining. In the 2014 study, nearly 9.5 percent of students said they "frequently" felt depressed – a figure that rose 3.4 percentage points since the 2009 study. [18]

I mentioned it earlier in the book, but a different study by the ACHA found that more than half of college students have experienced "overwhelming anxiety" sometime over the past year. More than 30 percent of them said they have felt so depressed "that it was difficult to function." Nearly 40 percent said they "felt things were hopeless." [19]

My friend, Julie Daubenspeck, is an author, speaker, counselor, and mom. She's one of the best listeners and just oozes love and compassion to anyone in pain. When I'm depressed, Julie is one of the first people I want to call. Like many powerful people in healing ministry, Julie's compassion was forged in the fires of suffering. I met Julie while speaking at the Hawaiian Islands Ministries (HIM) conference. After I was done speaking, she showed me a copy of the book she was writing called *Broken Treasures*. I'll never forget what Julie said that night,

"Christy, would you be willing to look at this book I'm writing? It's about my life and how I survived my childhood after being molested by my father."

Tears filled my eyes and I told her how sorry I was to hear about her painful childhood. With the purest, sweetest heart, Julie said to me, "It was very hard, but what the Enemy meant for evil, God is using for good. My book and ministry is helping girls overcome depression and find healing once they're broken." Julie completed her master's in marriage and family therapy degree, and is now working with domestic violence victims and counseling many young girls who have been sexually abused. God is using her powerfully to bring healing, hope, and freedom to hundreds of young women.

There are many depression tests you can find online, however, it's important to understand that you can't fully diagnose yourself as having depression from just taking home tests on your own. After consulting with licensed psychologists and psychiatrists, I'm including the following depression screening instrument below. Again, you can't fully diagnose depression in your life without some help from a doctor or counselor. But it's often helpful to better understand your feelings and how you might need help. If you go through the screening questions on the next page, and it looks like you do have symptoms of being depressed, I will give you some ideas about safe people you can contact who will help.

PATIENT HEALTH QUESTIONNAIRE-9
(PHQ-9)

Over the last 2 weeks, how often have you been bothered by any of the following problems?
(Use "☒" to indicate your answer)

	Not at all	Several days	More than half the days	Nearly every day
1. Little interest or pleasure in doing things	0	1	2	3
2. Feeling down, depressed, or hopeless	0	1	2	3
3. Trouble falling or staying asleep, or sleeping too much	0	1	2	3
4. Feeling tired or having little energy	0	1	2	3
5. Poor appetite or overeating	0	1	2	3
6. Feeling bad about yourself — or that you are a failure or have let yourself or your family down	0	1	2	3
7. Trouble concentrating on things, such as reading the newspaper or watching television	0	1	2	3
8. Moving or speaking so slowly that other people could have noticed? Or the opposite — being so fidgety or restless that you have been moving around a lot more than usual	0	1	2	3
9. Thoughts that you would be better off dead or of hurting yourself in some way	0	1	2	3

FOR OFFICE CODING ___0___ + _____ + _____ + _____

=Total Score: _____

If you checked off any problems, how difficult have these problems made it for you to do your work, take care of things at home, or get along with other people?

Not difficult at all	Somewhat difficult	Very difficult	Extremely difficult
☐	☐	☐	☐

Developed by Drs. Robert L. Spitzer, Janet B.W. Williams, Kurt Kroenke and colleagues, with an educational grant from Pfizer Inc. No permission required to reproduce, translate, display or distribute.

You can also learn more about depression by going to my website www.sayshutup.com. Under the media page, you will find a link to my HIM 2015 talk on Healing Depression. (BTW: I highly recommend Julie's book, *Broken Treasures*, which is now available on Kindle and online stores. It's extremely encouraging and healing for any young person who has been through sexual abuse. There's a link to the free download in our Appendix. Check it out!)

UNDERSTANDING ANXIETY

Remember Riley from the movie? Well, in Riley's brain, the feeling named Fear wasn't too loud inside her mind until her family moved and she started a new school. The first day at school, Fear was shouting inside her brain, which makes total sense given that she no longer felt safe since her best friends were far away.
The feeling, fear, can sometimes be our friend by warning us to stay away from danger. One day, my son Benji was playing basketball in our street. Sitting on the front porch, I noticed a red car speeding down the street, and I knew Benji didn't see it coming. While Benji was shooting the ball, my heart was racing with fear and I ran toward him, shouting,

"Benji! CAR! Get out of the street!" Benji turned and jumped out of the street just as this red car zoomed by – speeding way too fast in a neighborhood with children! That feeling of fear was my friend because it signaled danger and helped keep my son safe.

But feelings of fear aren't always friends. They are important to understand, but fear and anxiety can cripple your life. Anxiety can make you afraid of things that aren't real dangers. Anxiety can make your head hurt, your stomach upset, and your heart beat so fast you feel paralyzed (also called a panic or anxiety attack). Anxiety can become so overwhelming that it can be hard to function and go to school. Anxiety can cause insomnia and nightmares. For some people, anxiety can be phobias of certain things like spiders, airplanes, or the dark.

If you struggle with anxiety, you aren't alone. Do you know how many teens and college students are struggling with anxiety today? It's a large number of people in your generation. These statistics about anxiety among your peers should make you and your friends aware that you're not alone if you have anxiety. Keep in mind, that these numbers are probably low. These are only the teens and college students who are actually reporting their anxiety. You likely know that many of your friends are very anxious but just not telling anyone.

Check out what this article by the American Psychological Association (APA) said (and the table following shows) about anxiety:

> ...Almost half [of United States college students] said they felt overwhelming anxiety in the last year, according to the 2013 National College Health Assessment, which examined data from 125,000 students from more than 150 colleges and universities. [20]

And this:

> More than 30 percent of students who seek services for mental health issues report that they have seriously considered attempting suicide at some point in their lives, up from about 24 percent in 2010, says Pennsylvania State University psychologist Ben Locke, Ph.D., who directs the Center for Collegiate Mental Health (CCMH), an organization that gathers college mental health data from more than 263 college and university counseling or mental health centers. [21]

STUDENTS UNDER PRESSURE

College and university mental health trends by school year among students already receiving services at counseling centers.

	2010-11	2011-12	2012-13*
Attended counseling for mental health concerns	45.2%	47.6%	48.7%
Taken a medication for mental health concerns	31.0%	31.8%	32.9%
Been hospitalized for mental health concerns	7.0%	7.8%	10.3%
Purposely injured yourself without suicidal intent (e.g. cutting, hitting, burning, hair pulling, etc.)	21.8%	22.5%	23.2%
Seriously considered attempting suicide	23.8%	25.5%	30.3%
Made a suicide attempt	7.9%	8.0%	8.8%
Considered seriously hurting another person	7.8%	7.9%	11.2%
Intentionally caused serious injury to another person	2.4%	2.2%	3.3%

Source: Center for Collegiate Mental Health

*In 2012-13 the answer format was changed for all items except prior counseling/ medication. This change may have partially accounted for some of the increases, but because rates changed differentially, it's clearly more than that. For a more detailed explanation of changes, see the Center for Collegiate Mental Health 2013 Annual Report.

Everyone is afraid of something. But, when anxiety becomes the loudest voice in your brain, it can be hard to function and very hard to have joy because you're always afraid about what bad thing might happen next. If you are struggling with anxiety, there are things you can do that will help you overcome your worries. Listed below is a screening instrument for anxiety. Most teens and young adults score high on this anxiety-screening instrument given the pressures facing you guys today. The good news is that you can find help for your worries and anxious feelings. Take the screening test yourself, and then stay tuned for more help in chapter 9, "Find Safe People (Who Will Shut Up and Listen)."

Generalized Anxiety Disorder 7-item (GAD-7) scale

Over the last 2 weeks, how often have you been bothered by the following problems?	Not at all sure	Several days	Over half the days	Nearly every day
1. Feeling nervous, anxious, or on edge	0	1	2	3
2. Not being able to stop or control worrying	0	1	2	3
3. Worrying too much about different things	0	1	2	3
4. Trouble relaxing	0	1	2	3
5. Being so restless that it's hard to sit still	0	1	2	3
6. Becoming easily annoyed or irritable	0	1	2	3
7. Feeling afraid as if something awful might happen	0	1	2	3
Add the score for each column		+	+	+
Total Score *(add your column scores)* =				

If you checked off any problems, how difficult have these made it for you to do your work, take care of things at home, or get along with other people?

Not difficult at all _____
Somewhat difficult _____
Very difficult _____
Extremely difficult _____

Source: Spitzer RL, Kroenke K, Williams JBW, Lowe B. A brief measure for assessing generalized anxiety disorder. *Arch Inern Med.* 2006;166:1092-1097.

Your feelings really matter. You need to listen to them and part of how you will get better is by naming them, understanding them, and sharing them with safe people. *It's important to know that while your feelings matter they are not facts or reality.*

Many teens I encounter are suffering from depression or anxiety, and they don't understand that they can feel better. If you think you might be suffering from anxiety, depression, sadness, or hopelessness, please know this: You can be happy again. These feelings are temporary and there are many things you can do to move beyond these hard feelings to happy feelings like joy, happiness, peace, and love.

How can you do that? In the next chapter, we are going to talk about the negative thoughts inside your brain (these are different from your feelings). These thoughts can tear you down and make you feel bad about yourself. The good news: You can "shut up" those voices that are tearing you down and hear voices that build you up. When you shut up the bad voices inside your head and start hearing truth instead, it will be like walking out of a dark room into a place of light, happiness, and peace. Life is too short to let these negative, lying voices make you feel bad about yourself and hopeless about your future. You can feel happy again. Let's get started by discovering what voices inside your head are not your friends.

WHAT DO YOU THINK?

x   Did you see the movie *Inside Out*? If so, which character did you
    most relate to? (Joy, Sadness, Anger, Fear, or Disgust)

x   Most teens and college students have suffered from depression or
    anxiety at some point in their lives. Have you? Do you have other
    problems that are mentioned in this chapter that you want to
    talk about?

x   Did you take the Depression or Anxiety Screening test? Are you
    willing to share those results with your friend group? (P.S.: No
    one is allowed to judge you, and remember, this is a confidential
    group. Everyone is entitled to feel whatever he or she is feeling.
    No pressure to share your results if you're not comfortable!)

x   My son, Benji, sometimes struggles with worries, and he has a
    good way to handle it, saying, "Mom, I worry a lot, so I pray a lot."
    That's truly wisdom. I'd invite you right now to give your worries to
    God and ask for His peace to replace them.

CHAPTER 5

What Are The Bad Thoughts Inside Your Head?

X   Bad thoughts come in all different sizes and shapes. Some are dangerous and will threaten our very lives. Other bad thoughts just tear us down and make us feel bad about ourselves. Regardless, many of these bad thoughts are lies inside of our brain. They aren't true. Do you realize that the bad thoughts inside your head greatly influence how you think and feel? Did you ever wonder to yourself, *How did that voice get inside my mind? Is that thought even true?*

Understanding these different voices and learning what to do when you hear them is critical to your happiness. When you understand these voices, you can label them as truth or lies. Understanding the difference between these voices might just save your life.

When I talk with people in your generation, we have come up with four different kinds of voices we typically hear inside our heads.

WHAT ARE THE FOUR VOICES INSIDE YOUR HEAD?

1. Other people's voices (can be good or bad)
2. Your own voice (can be good or bad)
3. The Enemy's lying voice (always negative, bad, and destructive)
4. God's voice (always good)

What do these voices sound like? I'm going to describe each of these voices to you. As you read, I would encourage you to think about which voices you are hearing. Are they good voices, building you up? Or are they negative voices, tearing you down? In this chapter, we will focus on the first two of these four voices: (1) other people's voices and (2) your own voice.

In chapters six and seven, I will describe in detail the other two voices and how you can know the difference between the Enemy's lying voice and God's loving voice.

1. Other people's voices (good or bad)

Who are you hanging out with these days? What people are you communicating with most of the time? Parents? Teachers? Friends? Other people's voices echoing inside your head can be good or bad, depending on the people around you. The people you are surrounded by the most will impact what voices you're hearing inside your brain. If you are surrounded by kind, encouraging people who build you up, then you are likely to hear those uplifting voices in your head. But if the people talking to you are mean, shaming, or hurtful, those voices can get stuck in your head.

I don't have to tell you that bullying is a huge problem today in middle school, high school, and even college. The CDC defines bullying as this: "Any unwanted aggressive behavior(s) by another youth or group of youths, who are not siblings or current dating partners, involving an observed or perceived power imbalance and is repeated multiple times or is highly likely to be repeated." [22] The CDC also notes a few studies that say the following:

> Bullying may inflict harm or distress on the targeted youth including physical, psychological, social, or educational harm. [23] A young person can be a perpetrator, a victim, or both (also known as a "bully/victim").

> Bullying can occur in-person and through technology. Electronic aggression, or "cyber-bullying," is bullying that happens through email, chat rooms, instant message, a website, text message, or social media. [24]

Maybe you have experienced bullying yourself? No one should ever be allowed to bully you. When that happens, then those voices can get stuck inside your head, repeating themselves over and over like a bad video. Alyssa (a high school student) told me a sad story from her middle school years. One day in her seventh grade P.E. class, some girls laughed at her and started calling her "the fat girl." That bullying went on for months and those words were so hurtful that she would cry herself to sleep every night. She didn't tell anyone because she was afraid they would bully her more and she also felt ashamed of her body. In fact, she began to hate her body. Soon, Alyssa developed an eating disorder. Those mean words "fat girl" stuck in Alyssa's mind and became the loudest voices in her head. Over time, they became so loud that she ended up with an eating disorder that caused years of suffering for this sweet, beautiful girl.

Bullying is horrible. It's mean and cruel. Bullying should be stopped immediately when it's happening.

No one should be bullied in life. You deserve friends who build you up, not tear you down. If you are being bullied, I urge you to tell someone safe. I know it's hard, and it definitely takes courage. Many teens have told me that one of the reasons they don't tell their parents or teachers that they are being bullied is that they are afraid it will get worse. I understand it's risky to tell someone, but if you are being bullied, it must stop! God wants you to feel safe. I would encourage you to check out the website www.stopbullying.gov. You may find some ideas about what to do that will help you. Find a safe teacher, parent, pastor, or friend and tell him or her! Stand up for yourself because the bully hurting you should be shut down immediately.

When you are being bullied, those lies get stuck in your head. They can be very destructive. And here's the thing: Those lies are NOT the truth. If it's your "friends" doing this, then I'm going to tell you something that maybe hard for you to hear: You need to find new friends. Walk away from these people because they aren't really your friends; they are "frenemies." You deserve better. The friends God wants for you will build you up, not tear you down. These kinds of friends will say encouraging words to you, text you when you're down, and tell you that you're awesome. When you don't believe in yourself, they will believe in you.

What if the negative voices are coming from someone in authority like a teacher, parent, or relative? This is tricky, right? But it's still the same idea. God wants people to build you up, not tear you down. God wants you surrounded with people who believe in you, who say encouraging things to you and are your biggest cheerleaders. Now, I'm not here to bash parents. I'm a parent myself. I know most parents want you to have a better life than they did, and they want you to be successful and happy. I don't know your teacher or parents, so I'm not the judge. I love my kids like crazy and always try to say things that build them up, not tear them down. But I'm not perfect. I make mistakes. When I do, I try to go back to my kids and say something like,

"You guys when I got irritable and snapped at you, I was wrong. It wasn't your fault; it was mine. Please forgive me." My husband, Ben, taught me how to do this and calls this kind of apology a "fall on your sword." When we have conflict in our family, we teach our kids that saying the words "I'm sorry" is one of the strongest and wisest things you can do. It's a sign of strength not weakness. I believe that if more parents would model the incredible gift of saying the simple words, "I'm sorry. Please forgive me," countless marriages would be saved and not end up in divorce. Many parent-child relationships would be healed if we learned to be humble and say, "I'm sorry" more often. (Parents especially need to say this to kids! Let's model humility and forgiveness to our children.) If people learned how to be kind to one another and apologize (which Jesus taught us to do) many teens could grow up in happier homes, learning that no one is perfect and when we fail, we can find forgiveness instead of shame. No parent is perfect. But Jesus does want you to know that if you're hearing messages from your parents or teachers that are hurtful, shaming, negative, or tearing you down, that's not the voice of God.

Here is some good news for you. If you've been hurt by other people's words (no matter who they are), God can heal those wounds. Painful words can be like thorns in your heart, but God can pull those thorns out and tell you His truth that will heal those wounds. God wants to do that for you. You can silence those negative voices in your mind, and hear God's voice of love: *I made you. I love you. You are beautiful and I will always be with you and never leave you alone.*

2. Your own voice: How do you talk to yourself?

Do you look in the mirror and think to yourself, *Wow! I'm awesome! I am just beautiful!* Ha! Not many of us do, but I wish we did. Most people, especially teenagers, struggle with self-image. Every teenager I know can tell you about a part of their body or personality that they don't like.

It's one thing to wish you had longer hair, or a better nose, or that you were a faster runner. We all have those thoughts. But when our own voice is constantly ripping us apart inside, it's destructive. When our "self talk" becomes self-hatred, it's tragic. We can be our own worst enemies. We can bully ourselves! Usually when that is happening, it's because we've heard negative, shaming things from other people about ourselves. Then we start to believe the lies. I meet with hundreds of teenagers and young adults. Let me assure you that none of them is perfect. In fact, it's often the ones that seem to have it all together who are suffering inside. Insecure people often put other people down in order to feel better about themselves.

THE NEGATIVE VOICES CHECKLIST

What negative voices are you hearing inside your mind? Look at the checklist on the next page. It lists some of the negative voices and thoughts that many of my young friends have shared with me. As you read through it, please check any voices that sound familiar to you. Also check how often you're hearing that message or ones like it. This is a confidential checklist between you and God. Just fill it out and keep it right here. Later, you might choose to share it with a safe adult but that's up to you. (We will talk more about this in chapter nine about finding safe people.) The point of this checklist is to help you become aware of what negative words are rolling around inside your head. Often, bringing those voices "into the light" and out of your mind is helpful in and of itself. Becoming aware of them is the first step toward understanding them. Some of these voices are telling us important things (even if they are negative) and can ultimately help us. Other negative voices we need to simply get free from and shut them up in Jesus' name.

What negative messages are inside your head?
Check the ones you sometimes feel and how often you feel them.

	OFTEN	SOMETIMES	RARELY	NEVER
I'm ugly	○	○	○	○
I'm unlovable	○	○	○	○
I'm not good enough	○	○	○	○
I'm stupid	○	○	○	○
I'm fat	○	○	○	○
I hear voices telling me to throw up or stop eating	○	○	○	○
I feel scared most of the time	○	○	○	○
I feel sad	○	○	○	○
I feel alone	○	○	○	○
God doesn't love me	○	○	○	○
I feel hopeless	○	○	○	○
I hear voices saying I would be better off dead	○	○	○	○
I hear voices telling me to hurt myself	○	○	○	○
I hear voices telling me to kill myself	○	○	○	○

If you did the depression and anxiety screening tests (in the previous chapter) and scored high on those, or you did the negative thoughts checklist here (and checked more than five) you would benefit from talking with a safe professional. If you checked "often" on the last four questions on this list, you need to talk with a safe adult right now. (If you don't know a safe adult, check out chapter 9's "Safe People" list that has people available to talk with you immediately.) I know it's hard to trust other people, but you will find some ideas about safe people that I think might help in that chapter.

The purpose of this negative checklist is for you to become aware of how you're seeing yourself and what the negative messages are inside your head. These negative messages are lies. God wants to fill your head with loving, encouraging messages that build you up and make you feel good. My challenge to you is this: Be kind to yourself. Instead of beating yourself up, love yourself like you would love one of your best friends. Expose all the lies you're saying to yourself, and start celebrating all the good things about you. Right now, I want you to list five things you like about yourself (or positive things other people have said about you).

Five good things I like about myself or that I've heard others say about me:

1.

2.

3.

4.

5.

Five people I know who care about me:

1.

2.

3.

4.

5.

Five things I'm thankful for right now:

1.

2.

3.

4.

5.

If you have trouble finding five things you like about yourself, let me lovingly tell you that you're wrong. Because I feel certain that even though I don't know you, we all have positive qualities that we often don't see ourselves. In fact, I'm guessing that if I took you out to coffee for your favorite drink, and we spent an hour together, I could come up with at least five positive things about you. And, I don't even know you! I'm also sure that someone in your life cares about you and that person could list five good things about you. But if you can't do that, then for now, just notice how your own inner voice is very critical. That's the first step toward healing.

There are negative voices we all struggle with but there are also destructive, dark voices that are different from our negative thoughts. In the next chapter, I'll talk about where these dark, lying, destructive voices are coming from and how you can find power to shut them up.

WHAT DO YOU THINK?

x   Do you notice that other people's voices inside your head either build you up or tear you down?

x   How do you talk to yourself? Is your own voice critical or loving?

x   If you're meeting with a group, try this encouraging exercise: Everyone takes turn being the listener. Then, the other members of the group each take two minutes to say the positive qualities they see in you and what they like about you.

CHAPTER 6

What Does Your Enemy's Voice Sound Like?

X   The following story is a true story, but the names and some events have been changed to protect the identities of those involved.

One dark and rainy night in November, Michael made a plan to end his life. His parents had recently divorced, and then his girlfriend broke up with him. He became so depressed that he thought it would be better for everyone if he died. In Michael's own words,

"I don't think I really wanted to kill myself, I just couldn't shut up the voice inside my head." The next day, he went to school, planning to jump in front of the train that very night. Michael said he kept hearing this voice inside his brain saying, *Jump Michael! This pain will never stop and no one will miss you if you're dead anyway.* When the bell rang for lunch, Michael's basketball coach, Mr. Carter, surprised him by asking if he could take him out for burgers for lunch. (Mr. Carter said later that he noticed Michael looking sad and felt moved to reach out to him.) As they were eating their burgers and fries, Mr. Carter asked Michael how he was really doing, because he noticed that he seemed down lately. Michael opened up, and began sharing with Mr. Carter how depressed he had been feeling. Mr. Carter quietly listened, and then he told Michael how much he respected him and how sorry he was for all the pain. Michael became teary and admitted that he has been feeling so hopeless that he was planning to commit suicide. Mr. Carter told Michael that ending his life wouldn't fix things and that everyone would really miss him. He asked Michael if he had told his parents, and Michael said no, because he was ashamed. After lunch, Mr. Carter asked Michael if they could tell his parents together about how much pain he was in and get him some help. Michael agreed and with Mr. Carter's help, Michael told his parents about how depressed he was and that he had made plans to end his life. His parents were heartbroken and felt horrible that they didn't even see that their son was suffering and suicidal. Thankfully, his parents were kind and loving, and they helped him find a good counselor and also a young pastor who began to spend time with him, encouraging him and praying with him. Today, Michael is much better, and he says that he believes God sent that coach to save his life on that rainy day.

What voices were whispering inside Michael's head? Was the voice that told him he would be better off dead and that he should jump in front of the train just depression? Or was that a darker, more destructive voice trying to kill Michael?

This chapter is about spiritual warfare and those dark, lying, and demonic voices that are very real and want to harm you. The Bible talks about very real powers of good and evil in this world. You maybe surprised to hear this, but many adults (in our Western world) don't believe that "evil" is a real thing. People don't want to believe it's true. We live in a "you have to see it to believe it" kind of world that values scientific research and verifiable statistics you can see. But that's not true everywhere. There are many cultures where you don't have to convince people that there is good and evil in the world: They believe it already.

My experience talking with young people today is that the large majority of people in your generation believe in forces of good and evil. As you already know, we've talked with over a thousand and we have actually had input from over 350 about this specific question regarding spiritual warfare. The question? "Do you believe there is good and evil in the world?" Almost 93 percent of them said yes. We also asked on the quiz, "Do you believe that demons are real?" and 70 percent of people who responded replied yes, 15 percent said they didn't know, and only 5 percent said no.

Many teens and college students have privately told me that they think it's pretty ridiculous when therapists claim that mental illness is the only explanation for the epidemic of teenage suicide we are witnessing today. In fact, most young people I talk with believe that mental illness is only part of the problem. While mental illness might explain *some* of the epidemic of pain your generation is facing, I believe it's only part of the problem.

When I speak to large groups of teens and college students, I often ask them this question:

"How many of you know of someone who has committed suicide?" The large majority (over 85 percent) in every audience will answer yes. Then I tell them this: "Wow! When your parents and I were growing up, suicide among our friends or peers was unheard of."

This is the sad world you guys are growing up in today. You saw the statistics earlier. Can we really just explain all of this on depression or anxiety? After all, weren't people anxious, depressed, and mentally ill 20 years ago?

My teenager daughter, Corey, and my husband, Ben, went on a mission trip to Rwanda two years ago to learn about the genocide. Ben was a missionary in the Congo before the genocide, and he says that when the genocide broke out, people could no longer explain this evil mass murder of millions of people by saying mental illness caused it all. The genocide in Rwanda and Congo was literally neighbors killing neighbors with machetes and 16 years of violence that has resulted in over "5.4 million people dying which makes it the world's bloodiest war since World War II."[25] This kind of violence is hard to explain away by just saying people are depressed, angry, or mentally ill. This type of epidemic is so horrible that it makes no rational sense and just seems to point to the fact that there are forces of good and evil in this world.

Corey and Ben went to Rwanda last summer and stayed with our dear friend, and mentor, Archbishop E. M. Kolini. After the genocide, Kolini was asked by the Rwandan government to help put the country back together because he was one of the few men that both the Tutsi and Hutu tribes (those embroiled in the conflict) respected.

Corey interviewed victims of the genocide. One lady told her that she saw her own sister murdered by a family friend. Corey told me this once after taking it all in,

"Mom, what's happening to teens today isn't as violent and widespread as that horrific genocide, but I couldn't help thinking about the epidemic facing my generation today. My friends and I don't think that mental illness is completely responsible for all these suicides, cutting, or the depression we are seeing all around us. We also believe that the Enemy is targeting our generation and causing some students to cut themselves, jump off bridges, or shoot themselves. We live in a spiritual war zone ourselves."

I think Corey is right. My previous work in a counseling clinic taught me a lot about mental illness and the patients who are suffering from very real diagnosable mental illnesses. But I also believe that mental illness is only part of the problem we are witnessing among today's youth.

In the Bible, we are told about a very real Enemy. Maybe you never considered this biblical belief that there is an Enemy who is evil and dark with a mission to lie, kill, and destroy people. I invite you to consider what I'm about to tell you. Because if the Bible is true and you face a real Enemy, it's important that you understand how to protect yourself and your friends.

WHAT DOES THE BIBLE SAY ABOUT EVIL?

I could write a whole book about what the Bible says regarding the spiritual war that is operating in our world. If you read the Bible cover to cover, there is no doubt that there are forces of good and evil. The good news is that the Bible is full of hope and if we know the power God has given us, we don't need to be afraid. God gives us spiritual power to fight the Enemy. Let's start by looking at some of the passages in the Bible that talk about spiritual warfare and the dark voices we might hear:

> For our struggle is not against flesh and blood, but against the rulers, against the authorities, against the powers of this dark world and against the spiritual forces of evil in the heavenly realms. (Ephesians 6:12, NIV)

Here is what Jesus said about the Enemy, Satan, and the kind of stuff that he is always doing: (Jesus is talking to a demon here, by the way.)

> "You belong to your father, the devil, and you want to carry out your father's desires. He was a murderer from the beginning, not holding to the truth, for there is no truth in him. When he lies, he speaks his native language, for he is a liar and the father of lies." (John 8:44, NIV)

Then Jesus said this about the Enemy:

> "The thief comes only to steal and kill and destroy; I have come that they may have life, and have it to the full."
> (John 10:10, ESV)

The Bible says this:

> Be alert and of sober mind. Your Enemy the devil prowls around
> like a roaring lion looking for someone to devour.
> (1 Peter 5:8, NIV)

YOUR THOUGHTS?

What is your opinion about all this? When a voice says to someone, *Cut yourself, kill yourself, shoot yourself,* or *It would be better
for everyone if you were just dead,* is that purely mental illness or is
there something darker going on? Many psychologists would tell you
that mental illness is the reason teens are jumping in front of trains,
cutting themselves, shooting other kids on a bus or walking into a
church and killing people.

What's your opinion? I love hearing from teenagers when they email
me from all over the country. They are wise, perceptive, and have
great ideas. Let me know what you think? Can we really explain away
all the suffering your generation is facing with a mental illness label?
Do we really think that epidemic of teenage suicide, which is now
the second leading cause of death among teens 10 to 24, is only because kids are depressed? What do you think? I find that teens have
tremendous wisdom, and I would love to hear your opinion if you'll
contact me at christy@sayshutup.com.

I've promised you I would be honest about my opinion and not tone
things down. So, let me tell you what I've experienced first hand, and
my own thoughts about the Enemy's voice. Do I think the voices telling young people stuff like *You should just shoot yourself* are caused
entirely by mental illness? No. When psychologists tell us that mental
illness is 100 percent responsible for the level of teenage problems
we are seeing today, I disagree. Do I think mental illness is part of
it? Yes. Have I confused you yet? Hang on! As I've told you, I come
from a family of medical doctors. Many good doctors and counselors
have helped me personally in my lifetime. I'm a big believer in good
psychiatrists, doctors, and counselors. I like to tell people I have my
own Ph.D. in anxiety and depression. So, I'm not one of those people

who believes there is a demon behind every bush. At the same time, I know that most of our brothers and sisters in third-world countries have a worldview that absolutely believes there are demons and evil forces in the world.

Many good people are trying to help your generation overcome the negative and dark voices, but very few are talking about how to empower you to fight dark and demonic voices. If we believe the Bible is true, why aren't we equipping your generation to stand against the Enemy? If we were sending you into Afghanistan to fight a war, would we send you in without any weapons to defend yourself? No way! So, I want to risk making some people mad at me or thinking I'm a bit crazy, and tell you that I don't care what people think about me. My call is to help your generation find healing and freedom in Jesus' name. I want to help you figure out these things for yourself. If you have depression or anxiety, I will do my best to connect you to resources to help you with those problems. If you are being harassed by a demon, let's help you expose that liar and shut it up.

As I interview some of the best doctors and therapists I know, many of them (regardless of their religious views) privately tell me they think the suicide epidemic among your generation is not fully explainable by mental illness. I agree. Last month, a sweet girl that just left one of the best treatment centers in Alabama for teenage depression walked straight out of the hospital and jumped off a bridge. Two weeks ago, a young 23-year-old man, a teacher who knew about my book, called me requesting a meeting. Over coffee, he calmly told me that he just left a traumatic relationship. Apparently, his girlfriend pulled out a gun and tried to shoot him, and then shot herself and died. What the heck? This guy is one of the kindest, most caring teachers I've ever met. Interestingly, he told me that when she pointed that gun at him, he knew it wasn't her doing this, but something much darker had taken control of his girlfriend. (BTW, this man isn't a Christian.)

So, as I talk with teens and college students, and as I interview therapists in various cities, here is what I believe to be true: Yes, I believe there is an epidemic of mental illness. But when mental illness crosses over into other voices telling you to hurt yourself, I believe that those dark voices can be from the Enemy. They are the ones the Bible says have come to "steal, kill, and destroy" (John 10:10, ESV).

A good friend of mine works in a psychiatric ward with teenagers who are in a lockdown unit in the hospital. Some of the teenagers there report hearing voices telling them to cut themselves or kill themselves. In many psychiatric hospitals, these kids would immediately be diagnosed as psychotic or another mental illness diagnosis from the Diagnostic and Statistical Manual of Mental Disorders (DSM), that doctors and therapists use to diagnose mental illness. Doctors might say that a person hearing voices is suffering from something like a multiple personality disorder or schizophrenia. The person suffering will most likely be heavily medicated. (Sometimes medication is helpful, by the way, but it must be the right kind and carefully monitored especially when given to teenagers.) Some of these mental illness diagnoses might be right, but the problem is sometimes it's not right. And no amount of medication seems to stop the voices or help the person.

My friend (a Buddhist nurse) who works at a hospital unit treating these teens said to me recently,

"Christy, it's so awful. These kids will sometimes tell me that they feel the devil is tormenting them with these dark thoughts and they can't get him to shut up."

This makes me so sad. Some mental illness is very hard to heal. But shutting up the Enemy? That's not hard at all if you know what to do. We can help you shut up the dark voices with God's power. It's just not that hard.

SPIRITUAL WARFARE 101

I wish I had been given the opportunity to teach those courageous teenagers in that hospital about spiritual warfare. Since I can't talk with them directly, I'm writing to you guys. You see, it can be scary to feel powerless against dark forces in the world and believe that Satan is tormenting your mind. What I wish I could have told those young people is this: I believe you. I believe it when you tell me that you are hearing voices that are satanic. *But I would also tell them this: You don't need to be afraid. God will help you.* You don't have to give Satan that much power in your life, and God can give you the power to shut up those dark voices in Jesus' name. I would also help them understand that the Enemy is lying to them. First of all, the devil (the one the Bible calls Satan) isn't omnipresent like Jesus. That means Satan can only be in one place at a time. (Like maybe Satan was inside Hitler or the person who started the genocide in Africa.) Those tormenting voices you may hear are real but aren't likely to be Satan himself. Instead, those voices are his little workers called demons. These demons have a mission to lie, harass, bully, and torment people. They will try to get a person to harm themselves or others. If they can, their ultimate goal is to get a person to commit suicide or hurt someone else.

Demons try to act really big and powerful, but they aren't. They are actually similar to those ugly bugs called cockroaches. Yuck! I hate cockroaches because I think they're creepy. But I'm not afraid of them. I know I'm bigger and more powerful than they are. If I see a cockroach, I stomp on them and I don't have any guilt about stepping on one. (Sorry if you're a fan of the cockroach.)

Demons are like these nasty little bugs. They will try to make you feel powerless, but God can give you all the power you need to get rid of them. We will show you how to do that in chapter eight.

THE RELATIONSHIP OF MENTAL ILLNESS TO DEMONS

In the Pierce house, we have a small zoo: three cats, two dogs, and two parakeets, plus a few fish. (Your parents might say that I let my kids have too many pets, and they're probably right.) I would defend myself, though, and say that adopting one of our cats, Smokey, wasn't my fault. Several years ago, we were riding horses and a man in the barn came to us with a bucket full of two-week-old kittens. He told us the owner asked him to drown the kittens. Seriously? I'm surrounded with my crying kids and their friends, who are saying,

"Please don't let them die, Mommy. Jesus wouldn't let them die!" Long story short, we end up feeding these four little kittens with baby bottles, and Smokey has joined the ranks of our zoo animals (a few nice friends adopted the rest of them).

We love Smokey, and he's a boy cat. Boy cats are kind of like the big male lions you see in Africa. (Smokey even looks a little wild!) In Africa, the male lions often lie sleeping under the trees. The female lions are the real hunters. Our female cat, Pumpkin, is definitely the hunter in our cat family. One day, I was cooking tacos for dinner, and I heard the kids screaming in the other room. I ran into the living room and I immediately saw the problem. Pumpkin had proudly marched into our family room, where the kids were watching *Modern Family*, and she dropped a dead black rat at their feet. GROSS! Of course, we called Ben to get rid of it. (It was clearly a Daddy job.) When Ben went outside to throw away the dead rat, he noticed that a big can of garbage had been spilled in our alley. No wonder Pumpkin found a rat outside. You know the old saying, right? "Where there is garbage, there will be rats."

Rats and garbage is the perfect image when it comes to the relationship between demons and mental illness or emotional pain (my friend and mentor, Dr. Chuck Kraft, taught me about this in his book, *Defeating Dark Angels*.) Whenever I encounter a demon, I know that there is likely garbage there somewhere. I've been familiar with spiritual warfare now for over 20 years, and when I encounter someone being tormented by demonic voices, I always look for the reason the demons are there. Sometimes it's mental illness. The "garbage" can also be things like abuse, trauma, drugs, persistent sin (like porn), or other emotional pain. Involvement in satanic cults and/or witchcraft also opens a door to demonic harassment. Just because you have mental illness doesn't necessarily mean you will also have demonic oppression. But it makes you more vulnerable (especially if you stay alone and don't get help). So, when we hear about a teen or young adult shooting other people or themselves, I know that while it's likely mental illness is involved, that's not the whole story. There are even some mental health professionals who acknowledge something deeper – something spiritual – in the mix. In an opinion article published in *The Washington Post* titled, "As a Psychiatrist, I Diagnose Mental Illness. Also, I Help Spot Demon Possession," a New York-based psychiatrist (who, by the way, trained in psychiatry at Yale and in psychoanalysis at Columbia) explains that he believes many of his clients are antagonized by demons, and emphasizes it's important to consider both the mental and the spiritual when treating a patient.

"Those who dismiss these cases unwittingly prevent patients from receiving the help they desperately require," Dr. Richard Gallagher said, "either by failing to recommend them for psychiatric treatment (which most clearly need) or by not informing their spiritual ministers that something beyond a mental or other illness seems to be the issue." [26]

The mental illness is the garbage, but I believe that the rat is just another stupid demon that got a person to listen to the lie *kill yourself*, or *you would be better off dead.*

Now, this stuff can be a little freaky and get people all worried and scared about demons and darkness. *I invite you to listen to the tremendously good news: No demon has the right to harm you if you believe in Jesus.* In fact, when you put your faith in Jesus, the Holy Spirit comes and lives inside you. That means you are never alone. God is always with you, inside you, ready to protect you from anything dark or demonic. When you invite Jesus to become your God and protect you, the Holy Spirit, who lives inside you, is the same spirit that raised Jesus from the dead. That Holy Spirit inside you is way more powerful than Satan, much less those stupid cockroach-like demons.

God loves you more than you could possibly imagine. If you put your faith in Him, you are safe and protected. He can heal you from whatever mental illness, pain, and suffering you have endured. God wants you to experience His loving presence more in your life and learn how to use the spiritual power He has already given you. How can you do that? The next chapter is the key to shutting up the negative and dark voices that tear us down. Actually, it's the most important voice you need to hear because when you hear this voice speaking to you, it changes everything. When you hear this voice, you begin to understand that you are safe, protected, and have all the power you need to shut up the Enemy.

WHAT DO YOU THINK?

x Read this Bible verse where Jesus is talking about the Enemy and his demons:

"The thief comes only to steal and kill and destroy; I have come that they may have life, and have it to the full" (John 10:10, ESV).

x Do you believe that mental illness is fully responsible for people cutting themselves, shooting themselves or another person, or jumping in front of a train?

x Do you feel afraid of the Enemy?

x How can you feel safe and protected by God so you don't need to be afraid?

Prayer of Protection
You can pray this or have someone in your group say this prayer.

"Jesus, thank you that you have given us power to shut up the Enemy. Thank you that if we believe in you, you have made us children of God and we don't need to be afraid because we are protected by You. In Jesus' name, I declare myself and my friends off-limits to the Enemy's attacks and we forbid the Enemy from harming any of us. In Jesus' name, we call upon your angels to surround us all, and give us your peace now. Amen."

The next chapter will *encourage and empower you* that you can have spiritual power to shut up the Enemy's voice!

CHAPTER 7

What Does God's Voice Sound Like?

X   When my daughter Corey was four years old, I heard her singing in the backyard. Standing at the kitchen sink washing the dinner dishes, I heard her little voice drifting through the kitchen window singing this sweet little song,

"God I love the birds! I love the bees! I love the sky, but you tell me the truth: You love me!"

Something about that simple, beautiful song drew me, so I put down the kitchen towel and went outside into the yard. Corey was completely unaware of my presence, and she kept joyfully dancing and singing, so I just watched her. Finally, I got her attention and asked,

"Corey, honey, that song is just beautiful! Did you learn that at church?" She turned to me and said in a matter-of-fact voice something I will never forget:

"Oh no, Mommy. I didn't learn that at church. Nobody taught it to me. It's a special song that Jesus just put into my heart." She paused, looked up at the sky, smiled, and said, "I think it's because I'm God's special kid." That moment is forever etched in my soul because I knew that the Spirit of God had, in some very real way, gotten through to a four-year-old little girl the truth: She was God's special kid.

The most important voice that you need to hear in your mind is the loving voice of God. Do you have any idea how much God loves you? Whatever your personal experience of God's love is so far in your life, I can promise you this: God loves you more than you have ever experienced or imagined. His love for you is real. It is deeper and bigger than your wildest dreams. His love is able to overcome any obstacles you face in life. More than any other thing God wants to say to you, He wants you to hear his loud call: *I am with you. I am for you. I am trying to get through to you how much I adore you.*

The problem is that no matter how much we have heard people tell us, "God loves you," we do not always believe it. In fact, we hardly ever believe it. My friend Jordan Seng has this funny way he speaks on this truth. He always starts by saying,

"Before I begin speaking, there is something you need to know about me." Then he pauses, and looks up, and says with a twinkle in his eye, "I'm God's favorite person. You might be God's second favorite person, but I'm really His favorite." His point is simple: When we understand and believe in our identity as God's favorite kid, we are unstoppable.

When Benji was a toddler, I would strap him into his car seat, kiss him on the forehead, and with a big smile on my face, I would ask him this question:

"Benji, who is Mom's special boy?" He would get a big smile on his face and shout with joy,

"It's me, Mom!"

Today, Benji doesn't think it's too cool when I drop him at middle school and ask him the same thing. (Ha! I'm guessing you wouldn't either!) Still, I won't ever stop asking Benji that question, no matter how old he gets, because I want him to know that he is precious to me forever. He needs to know how much I love him.

God wants you to know that you are very special to Him. In God's eyes, you are beautiful. He has a good plan for your life and whatever pain you might be experiencing right now, God can heal you and give you a happy, good future if you turn to Him for help.

When you hear God whispering messages of love to your heart, all of life is changed. You have power to overcome the big problems you face because you know, not just in your head but also in your heart, that God loves you more than you ever understood before. The love of God becomes a very personal, real experience that's not just an idea but also a reality you experience deep inside your soul. None of us can fully comprehend it; there is always more. In the words of Paul in Ephesians, Jesus wants us to grasp "how wide and long and high and deep is the love of Christ" (3:18, NIV). God wants you to know this kind of love. It is not just head knowledge that God is trying to get through to you; it is a deep, heart-level experience that the God of the Universe is head over heels in love with you. It doesn't matter how weak, broken, or sinful you may be, and it doesn't even matter if you feel close to God: It's the real truth. When you get it that God loves you that much, you have more strength to fight life's battles. You operate from a place of safety and in a cocoon of love, knowing that God is really with you.

When the reality of God's incredible love penetrates our doubts and fears, and takes root in our soul, we are filled with an "I can" attitude, instead of the "I can't" one. For when you know that He is with you and He loves you, you really can do "all things through [Christ] who gives me strength" (Philippians 4:13, NIV).

More than any other message God wants to get through, not just to your head, but also to your heart, is how much He loves you. In fact, I think that is the whole reason the Lord made it possible to hear His whispering voice through the Holy Spirit! Life is dang hard enough. We are no longer bound up by fear, pain, and disbelief when the God of all creation breaks into our world with a shout of His love into our daily life. Through the Holy Spirit, we can actually hear God's whispering voice in a way that penetrates our hearts, so that we can exclaim, "God is REAL. He is HERE, and I never knew He loved me that much!"

DO YOU KNOW WHO YOU ARE?

It seems like a simple question. And yet, it's very hard to answer sometimes. I'm guessing that many of you often feel valued for what you do, not for who you are, right? The world tells you that you're valued if you make good grades, get into a good college, look pretty, date a hot guy (or girl), have cool clothes, do well in sports, get a good job....and the list goes on and on and on. But here is the truth: *You have tremendous value because of who you are, not because of what you do or how you look.* Regardless of how you might feel right now in your life, God is saying to you, *You are my child. You are deeply loved, and I know every worry, dream, and desire in your heart.* In Romans 8:14-17, God says this about those who put their faith in Jesus:

> *Because those who are led by the Spirit of God are children of God. For you did not receive a spirit that makes you a slave again to fear, but you received the Spirit of adoption. And by him we cry, 'Abba, Father.' The Spirit himself testifies with our spirit that we are God's children. Now if we are children, then we are heirs—heirs of God and co-heirs with Christ, if indeed we share in his sufferings in order that we may also share in his glory. (NIV)*

THE BIBLE AND YOUR TRUE IDENTITY AS GOD'S CHILD

When you read your Bible, you will see many verses reminding you about the truth of your true identity as God's child. Here are just a few of the many verses in the Bible that declare this truth:

You are God's child.

Now if we are children, then we are heirs—heirs of God and co-heirs with Christ. If indeed we share in His sufferings in order that we may also share with His glory.
(Romans 8:17, NIV)

You are a new creation in Christ!

So if anyone is in Christ, there is a new creation: everything old has passed away; see, everything has become new!
(2 Corinthians 5:17, NRSV)

God chose you.

"You did not choose me, but I chose you and appointed you so that you might go and bear fruit—fruit that will last—and so that whatever you ask in my name the Father will give you."
(John 15:16, NIV)

You are reconciled in Christ!

All this is from God, who reconciled us to himself through Christ and gave us the ministry of reconciliation: that God was reconciling the world to himself in Christ, not counting people's sins against them. And he has committed to us the message of reconciliation. (2 Corinthians 5:18-19, NIV)

God sees you through His eyes: righteous and holy.

...and to put on the new self, created to be like God in true righteousness and holiness. (Ephesians 4:24, NIV)

You have been born again by the Holy Spirit.

Jesus answered, "Very truly I tell you, no one can enter the kingdom of God without being born of water and spirit."
(John 3:5, NRSV)

You are a child of the light and don't belong to darkness.

You are all children of the light and children of the day. We do not belong to the night or to the darkness.
(1 Thessalonians 5:5, NIV)

You are saved by God's love and grace, not because of your performance.

God saved you by his grace when you believed. And you can't take credit for this; it is a gift from God. (Ephesians 2:8, ESV)

You are a conqueror.

No, in all these things we are more than conquerors through him who loved us. (Romans 8:37, NIV)

You have a calling from God.

Therefore, holy brothers and sisters, who share in the heavenly calling, fix your thoughts on Jesus, whom we acknowledge as our apostle and high priest. (Hebrews 3:1, NIV)

God has unique things planned for you.

For we are God's handiwork, created in Christ Jesus to do good works, which God prepared in advance for us to do. (Ephesians 2:10, NIV)

Silencing the negative and dark voices inside your head isn't that hard when you realize how much God loves you, and you understand that He's given you spiritual power. But you can't do that in your own strength. When you hear the loving, kind, and gentle voice of the Spirit of God saying to you, *I love you just the way you are. You don't have to do anything to earn my love or approval. I love you in spite of your mistakes and your imperfections. You are loved for who you are, not for what you do.* The Holy Spirit is also whispering to you messages of peace, not stress, and says, *Don't be afraid because I'm with you. You are loved and safe in My Presence. Those lying, dark voices have no power over you if you draw near to Me.*

If you believe in Jesus, you never have to be afraid. God wants to hold you in His safe arms, and give you His power to silence the Enemy's voice. If you've already asked Jesus to come into your life, ask God to turn up the volume on His voice that you can hear Him more clearly. A good prayer to pray is this: "God give me eyes to see myself like you see me."

I promised you at the start of this book I would be real with you, so I will tell you something directly. ***There is nothing I could say in this book that's more important than this: God loves you more than you could possibly imagine and you can hear the loving voice of God for yourself.***

Jesus is the only voice that you really need. If you have the Spirit of the Living God whispering inside your mind, if you learn to hear His loving voice, all the other negative voices will become less powerful in your mind. The more you experience His love, the less you will hear the lying voice of the Enemy. God wants to shut up those voices inside your mind that are tearing you down.

God loves you whether you know that or not. God loves you in spite of what you've done in life. God loves you even if you don't love or believe in Him. But, if you want a close, personal relationship with God, I want to give you an opportunity to invite Jesus into your heart and mind. People try to make this really complicated, and it's not. It's between you and Jesus. You don't need to be religious or have it all together. Instead, Jesus is waiting with open arms, for anyone who admits they aren't perfect and need Him. It's easy. My friend Margee says she doesn't really know how to pray but that she just talks to God. Awesome! That's exactly right. You don't need to know how to pray, you can just talk to God in your own words. Invite God (in your own words) to come into your life and forgive you for anything you've done wrong in life. (God promises to do that and wash you clean!) Ask God to take over and protect you. It's that simple, and yet that powerful. You can now experience God's presence and power with you, because God lives inside of you. You are really and truly not alone. God is with you.

A few of my teenage friends who helped me write this book thought it might be helpful to share the prayer that they prayed when they invited Jesus into their lives. There is nothing magical about this prayer, and you don't have to say certain words. But some people like to have a prayer to read, so I've written their prayer down below and you're welcome to pray this for yourself. Or make up your own prayer!

"Jesus, I need you. I want to hear Your voice in my life, and I need your power to shut up the negative voices that are inside my mind. Come Holy Spirit and take over my thoughts and heart. Help me know that I'm your special kid and that you love me. In Jesus' name, Amen."

You belong to God. You are His special kid. This is your new identity and the Enemy has no power over you anymore. Now let's talk about how you can use the power God has given you to shut up those negative voices.

WHAT DO YOU THINK?

x Do you believe that you are God's special kid?

x Did you realize that if you put your faith in Jesus, you are adopted into God's family and are safe in Him?

x Pray this prayer: "God give me eyes to see myself like you see me."

CHAPTER 8

Tell That Lying Enemy to Shut Up!

X   Most teens and young adults I know are skeptical of adults who say they "totally get it" when it comes to their problems. They are right. The truth is that nobody can fully understand what you're going through, except for Jesus. So, I won't insult you and pretend I have easy answers for why hard things happen in life.

I went through a very painful time in my life when I was your age. I would never want to go through it again, but I'm thankful for it. Sound weird? I'm going to share some of my painful story because I hope it will encourage you that even though God doesn't cause pain, He doesn't waste it. God really can take all the bad stuff in your life, and bring you to a happy place, and even use you to help others. It can happen. God does this kind of thing all the time.

When I was your age, I wanted to give up. The Enemy tried to kill my family and get us to abandon our faith. This is the year I say I "got my Ph.D. in suffering," and, honestly, I'm truly grateful for it now. In fact, I never would have experienced the loving Presence and power of God, and I never would have learned how to tell the Enemy to "shut up" if I hadn't walked through this hard time.

MY SISTER WAS BITTEN BY A COPPERHEAD SNAKE AND THEN STRUCK BY LIGHTNING...

Yep. True story. Here's how it happened. My sister, Amy, was just fresh out of college, and one night she was hanging out in a nice little park near our house, and she stepped on a rock and was bitten (on the heel) by a copperhead snake. She was rushed to the emergency room, and the doctor on call asked her,

"Amy, did you bring the snake with you?" WHAT? Through the blinding pain in her leg, Amy tried to explain politely that she didn't have a pet snake, but was bitten by a poisonous snake. Apparently, the ER doctor wasn't completely crazy, because at that time, they didn't give the anti-venom medication unless they were sure the snake had a bacteria infection. Whatever. The bottom line is that my poor sister wasn't just bitten by a poisonous snake, but a sick poisonous snake. Amy was terribly sick the next year, often rushed to the emergency room with yet another life threatening infection, as the venom seemed to be attacking various organs in her body.

She eventually recovered and a year later, she got a job in a radio station as the local news broadcaster for the Ozark Mountains in Missouri. One morning in the Ozarks, there were thunderstorm and lightning warnings as my sister drove into the radio station to do the morning news. When she got to the radio station, she entered the sound booth to report the news, and she put her headphones on her head, turned on the power, and said,

"Good Morning, I'm Amy Varney. Here is the news today." At that very moment, a bolt of lightning struck the radio tower and Amy screamed as the electric currents powered into her headset. She threw off the headphones but was burned on her face. Yes, that's right. Amy was struck by lightning.

In my experience, people in crisis can either laugh or cry. My family is very close, and we kept going by laughing. In fact, my brother, Brian, who's from the Midwest and has a very dry sense of humor, told her,

"Well, Amy, I guess you're still good for some things, like jump-starting cars and stuff like that."

Could things get worse? Yes. A month later, Amy was driving to our house in another rainstorm in the dark. At that time, we lived by a small creek that was bordered by a field. When Amy's car came over the hill, she went down and heard a loud splash. To her horror, she discovered that the creek had turned into a river and her car was now floating in a flash flood. She opened the door and as water rushed inside the car, she stepped into water that was up to her waist. Walking in the dark through waist-deep water, she managed to walk safely to dry ground.

Amy: bitten by a poisonous snake, struck by lightning, washed away by a flash flood. Seriously! My family was desperate for prayer. It wasn't enough to know that God loved us though it was true. No, we needed more. We needed to experience God's presence and power with us. We needed to know that God was real and that He loved us.

So, we went to church after church asking people to pray for us. We didn't care what people thought. We just showed up and said,

"Hey, we've been having a few problems lately and if you have prayer teams around, we would be willing to receive prayer." One night, we showed up to a church where we didn't know a soul. At the end of the service, we were told that there was this guy with a gift of hearing God. When the service was over, we practically ran to see this guy. We got in a line of people waiting for him to pray for them. When it was our turn, he looked at Amy and said these words (no kidding),

"I'm glad you came up to see me. When I looked out at the audience tonight, I knew I needed to pray for you. Last night, I had a dream that a demon was chasing me, and the demon was in the form of a snake. On the head of the snake, the word, 'Copper' was written. Does that mean anything to you?" We were stunned. What became clear that night was that the things happening in our lives were not just random events, but that the Enemy was targeting my sister for some reason. Apparently, she was a threat, and the Enemy was doing everything to try and kill her. The Bible says, "As for you, you meant evil against me, but God meant it for good" (Genesis 50:20, NIV). That became true for our family. In our case, the Enemy targeted Amy for evil, but God used it for good. You see, my sister was the first one to become a Christian in our family. She prayed for all of us to become Christ followers. Eventually, all five of our family members became involved in Christian ministries. Not only that, the Enemy's constant attack drove us into the arms of a loving God. We began to experience the biblical truth of God's love for us in extraordinary ways. We learned how to hear God's voice, how to pray for healing, and how to do spiritual warfare. While I wouldn't like to repeat those years (especially for my sister), I don't regret them. Most of what I learned about the reality of God's love and power, I learned in that fire of suffering.

One night when I was desperate and angry with God, I went to bed crying. It had been weeks since I had slept through the night and I was exhausted. I got into bed and for some reason I don't fully under-stand, I said in a very angry voice this prayer:

"Father, Son and Holy Spirit, if you are real, prove it!" As I was falling asleep, I had one of the first dreams I ever had that I knew was from God. As I fell asleep crying, I dreamed that I was clinging to a rock on a mountain crying, and Jesus came. He picked me up, and took me into a cave in the mountainside. Inside the cave, he shut the door and covered me up with a blanket. He shut the door of the cave and by that I knew that I was completely safe and protected by God. That morning I woke up completely rested and full of peace. For the first

time in months, I had slept like a baby. For the first time in a long
while, I had hope.

That is my prayer for each of you reading this book – that you find
hope as you experience the love and very near presence of Jesus
through the Holy Spirit. I pray that you would understand (not just in
your mind, but in your heart) that God is real and that He loves you.
Maybe you are in a desperate place, like I was that night in my bed
crying, and you need to pray, "Father, Son, and Holy Spirit, if you are
real, show up." I don't know how God will answer that prayer for you.
Most likely, it will be different than how God answered me that warm
night years ago. But I know that God loves you more than you can
ever imagine, and He knows how to get through to you.

I'm going to end this chapter with some very practical things that
have helped me hear God's voice and shut up the Enemy. I hope they
will encourage you that you can hear God's voice for yourself and
then silence the bad voices in His name.

**1. Remember who you are! You are God's special kid and He has
given you spiritual power.**

Before you can tell the Enemy to shut up, you need to remember who
you are. The power to shut up the Enemy comes from a very personal,
real relationship with the Living God.

My kids will tell you that I am a terrible camper. I'll admit it. I'm not
an outdoorsy kind of person. So when my husband invited me to
go on a mission trip to India, you can imagine I was pretty nervous.
Honestly, I was worried about the poverty we would see in India and
pictured starving, sad children. On the plane flying in, Ben explained
to me what we were about to witness. He told me about the untouchables, a people group in India that the government claims number
about 200 million. You may know that since Gandhi came to India,
the caste system was supposed to be destroyed. Everyone who lives
in India knows this just is not true. The caste system is still very much
operating in India on a day-to-day basis. The fact is, it is hard to
change a paradigm that has been around for thousands of years.

In India, an untouchable person is expected to know their place in life. That means they are not only poor, but they are the modern-day lepers we picture in the Bible: untouchable, unclean, unsafe. An untouchable has a life-long job of carrying dead bodies and cleaning the latrines. They live on the open sewers of India, sleeping alongside the pigs. Walking the streets of India, if you were to see one of the untouchables, you would not know it by his or her size or color. You would know his position in the caste by how he reacts to you. An untouchable would cover his head in shame and erase his footprints near you, for he is taught that his touch defiles other people. He is of less worth than animals. In fact, if an untouchable tries to enter a Hindu temple or Moslem mosque, he or she risks death. It is a horrible life of unimaginable suffering and shame that few of us have ever encountered. God has done a powerful work among the untouchables through a ministry started by Philip Prasad and his wife, Elizabeth, which has led well over a million people to Christ in the past 20 years alone.

The first day of our trip to India, we rode in a bouncy Jeep through the dusty streets of India, over ditches in the road and alongside people on bicycles or donkeys. It was crazy. We entered the first village where we were to meet the untouchables, and Philip told me a pastor had been there for about six weeks telling people about Jesus. Pulling up to our stop, a drove of pigs scattered to make way for our car. I could see the open sewers flowing with human waste. I closed my eyes and asked Jesus to help me reach out to people in such poverty. My heart burdened by the background of stench and poverty, I was blown away with what I saw when I climbed out of the Jeep: Children were rushing to greet us, with joy and huge smiles on their faces, as they shouted to us,

"Jamaseekee! Jamaseekee!" a saying that means "Victory to Jesus!" Several little children grabbed our hands and began to pull us into their humble little huts along the open sewer banks. We sat down on dirt floors, and they began to sing, "For thousands of years, the Hindus have made us dance like monkeys, but Jesus has come and given us new life." I could only stare in awe at the clearest picture of transformation I had ever seen, with these faces of joy before me, dirty pigs and rivers of human waste behind them. After they stopped singing, Philip stood up and said,

"And now, Christy will preach the Word of God to us." I was stunned. He did not warn me ahead of time that I would be speaking, and I was frankly so overwhelmed with the faith of these untouchable people, that I felt completely unworthy to speak anything to them. So, I stood up, and looked out at these dear people, and said the first thing that came to my mind:

"Jesus came to a village much like yours, and He said, 'Let the little children come to me.'" I paused, gaining composure, "Do you know why Jesus said that?" I did not expect an answer at all, and was planning to continue, but a little boy in the back, about nine years old, raised his hand. Everyone was surprised and turned to stare at this little boy. Philip motioned for him to stand up. He stood up tall in front of his village with tattered clothes, and his dirt-stained legs and bare feet, and he looked me straight in the eye, and said in a proud, bold voice,

"Jesus said, 'Let the little children come to me' because to us belong the Kingdom of heaven!" Tears began to stream down my face, and I sat down, unable to go on. (Thankfully, Philip took over the preaching from there!) No matter where I travel, I know I will never, ever forget that little boy. The love of Jesus radiated from his face in the most pure, powerful way I had ever seen. Even though he had only known Jesus a few short weeks, he had hold of the Truth. He knew that Jesus, the Creator of the Universe, loved him, an untouchable, with a love stronger than the oppressive caste system that defined him, deeper than the identity of trash that branded him, wider than the reaches of his poverty, and longer than the span of hardship and struggle he was sure to face.

My dear friend, Philip, one of the most amazing men of God I'll ever know, went to be with Jesus on May 30, 2016. I can only imagine the joy on Jesus' faith when he welcomed his son, Philip, into his forever home in heaven. Because of Philip's ministry, millions of untouchables will be in heaven with him one day.

Do you have any idea how much God loves you? Whatever your personal experience of God's love is so far in your life, I can promise you this: God loves you more than you have ever experienced or imagined. My prayer for you is that you remember who you are! You are a child of God. As my Annie once said,

"Mom, that's pretty cool. Like we are royalty, right?" Yep, that's right Annie. Remember that. When you believe in Jesus, you are adopted into God's family. You are a prince or princess and deeply loved by your Father in heaven.

2. Drag the Enemy's lies into God's light

We all have at least one lie we believe about ourselves. What are the lies that the Enemy is whispering to you? Do you know? The Enemy's goal is to get you to hate yourself and see yourself in a negative way. God wants to destroy those lies and help you see the truth about who you really are.

My friend Philip who worked with the untouchables once told me a story of a tradition among the untouchables that is a vivid example of destroying the lies we believe about ourselves and claiming the truth of who we really are in Jesus. Philip said,

"Christy, when an untouchable becomes a follower of Jesus, we have a new name ceremony. You see, untouchables are given a name at birth by those who oppress them. Their names are shaming and cruel. These names are given to them by oppressors and are meant to destroy their self-esteem. It's hard to believe that cruel people would give these untouchable children names like "Dirty," "Stupid," or "Cow Dung." When they are born, however, that's exactly what happens. When these untouchable people become Christians, one of the most powerful ceremonies is literally life changing. At the Name Changing Ceremony, the untouchable burns the old degrading names and they are given a new name like "Beautiful," "Son of God," or "Daughter of the King." Tears ran down my face as I listened to how these beautiful people embody the love of Jesus by literally changing their names.

What are the lies the Enemy is whispering inside your mind? What are the bad names the Enemy is putting inside your head that need to be burned? Take a minute now and close your eyes. Ask the Holy Spirit to reveal those lies right now. Write down any negative shaming names that the Enemy has been saying to you about yourself. Sometimes you'll notice that the mean lies you believe about yourself are because someone else said them to you. Let's burn those old names! "Fat," "Stupid," "Ugly," "Wimpy," "Idiot"...what are they? Don't you see! These mean, degrading names are all from the Enemy, no matter who said them. We need to drag them into the light and destroy them. Let's ask the Holy Spirit to give us our own name ceremony and replace the old names with His new beautiful ones.

Remember that old saying, "Sticks and stones may break your bones, but words will never hurt you"? It's not true. Remember Ashley had "fat girl" stuck in her mind from middle school. Bad names can stick with you and totally affect how you see yourself. "Wimp," "Stupid," "Weak," "Baby," "Ugly," and "Loser" are some common bad names kids hear that stay stuck in their mind. These are the lies the Enemy wants you to believe about yourself. What are the old, negative names a bully maybe called you? Are there any names that are stuck in your mind that are shaming and destructive to you?

Write down here any mean or shaming names that people have said to you or that you have said about yourself:

If you remembered some bad names that someone else put on you, or you put on yourself, good for you! The first step is exposing them and then we can get rid of them.

If you were here with me in California, I could take you to the beach, build a large bonfire, and burn those old names! But I'm not with you right now, so I have another idea. Go get a red sharpie or pen, and then come back to this page in the book. Take that red pen and write in capital letters, "SHUT UP!" across the top of those old bad names. These are lies that you've believed about yourself. We need to expose and shut up those lies because they are not true and they can no longer define you. Here's an example of what my high school friend, Stephanie, did in her book:

Stephanie's List:

"I wrote down the bad names that people have called me or I have believed about myself. As I wrote them, I realized these were lies of the Enemy, and it made me angry! So, I grabbed a red marker from my backpack, and I wrote the words SHUT UP over these names. It felt so good to see those lies on paper, then picture them crossed out, silenced in my mind and then choose to believe the truth of who I really am."

Stephanie's Example:

I'm going to invite you to do a little Holy Spirit experiment. Right now, take a minute and ask God to help you throw out the old names, and then give you a new name to replace the old lies of the Enemy. You can do that in your own words, or say the prayer I've written down below:

"Jesus, you see all the old names I have stuck in my mind from the lies people have spoken to me. I renounce those lies in Jesus' name. God,

I need you to speak the truth of who I really am. Give me a new name to replace the old lies. In Jesus' name I pray. Amen."

HOLY SPIRIT EXPERIMENT

This is a fun Holy Spirit experiment you can try. (Think of it like a fun lab instead of that chemistry lab you're sick of doing.) I invite you to close your eyes and ask God to communicate with you, in a way that only you can understand, the truth of how He sees you. Ask God to whisper a new name into your mind. Maybe you would like to play your favorite worship (or other uplifting music) or go to a place where you feel peace (a hike, a beach, a park). Ask God to start speaking to your mind the truth of who you are. Pay attention! The Spirit of God might download a very quiet whisper into your brain, and you might just hear God whisper to you a new name. You might have a picture drop into your mind. (One girl told me she saw a very faint picture of herself in a white dress with flowers in her hair holding Jesus' hand.) It may be a Scripture that comes to you. (One young guy told me he heard the Scripture, "*This is my son and with him I am well pleased,*" which moved him to tears because he never felt his dad was pleased with him.) If God speaks to you in nature, it might be a beautiful sunset or animal that shows up in an unusual way where you sense God is near to you.

If you don't hear anything at all, don't worry. And don't let the stupid Enemy lie to you that it's because this isn't real or you aren't special to God. (If you happen to hear something negative, that's either your own negative voice talking to you or the Enemy, so tell that voice to shut up!) Sometimes it takes a little time to learn how to quiet the noise in your head so you can hear the voice of God.

In my other book *God is Whispering to You* there are specific exercises to help you experience God's presence and peace. The book will help you learn to hear the loving voice of Jesus in more personal, real ways that make sense to you. Teenagers and young adults are using the book as a guide to hearing God and some are starting listening prayer groups. They are saying to us that when they start hearing God's voice personally for themselves, all of life looks different. They have hope and encouragement. Our staff and ministry Board want to get this book to every teen or young adult who wants to learn how to hear God's voice. If you can afford to buy a copy, that's great. It's available in hardcopy form or in a digital edition. You can find the book on Kindle and online stores or go to my website (again it's www.christypierce.org) where there is a link to buy the book. However, I want all young people who can't afford a copy to get one. We have some wonderful people who've donated money to make these books available to youth. Email Julie if you want a book at info@sayshutup.com.

3. Tell those negative voices and your Enemy to shut up in Jesus' name!

Jesus actually said the words "shut up." He really did. It may not sound like something Jesus would say, but it's true. What's awesome is that Jesus says it to a demon! And that stupid demon immediately shuts up. Very cool. Check out this verse and see what I mean:

> They went to Capernaum, and when the Sabbath came, Jesus went into the synagogue and began to teach. The people were amazed at his teaching, because he taught them as one who had authority, not as the teachers of the law. Just then a man in their synagogue who was possessed by an impure spirit cried out, "What do you want with us, Jesus of Nazareth? Have you come to destroy us? I know who you are—the Holy One of God!"

> "Be quiet!" said Jesus sternly. "Come out of him!" The impure spirit shook the man violently and came out of him with a shriek. (Mark 1:21-28, NIV)

The words "be quiet" can literally be translated from the original Greek to the words "shut up." In fact, Jesus was speaking pretty sternly to that demon and so I think "shut up" is a more accurate translation. Jesus wasn't being friendly. He was commanding that demon to immediately stop talking and be silent. Then Jesus commanded it to leave that man, and it did. Right away. Pretty cool.

Please don't tell your parents I said it's OK to sternly shout "shut up" at your brother or sister. Ha! But I do want you to understand that God has given you His power to shut up the voice of the Enemy. God has given you authority to say shut up to the negative and dark voices that are harassing your mind. You don't have to listen to them. You may feel powerless, but you're not. God has given you His power and authority to shut up the lying voice of the Enemy.

As a Christ follower, you are on the winning side. Jesus has already won the war. He came to earth, died on the cross, descended into hell, defeated Satan, rose again, and is seated at the right hand of the Father. Remember, you are His special kid. Your Father in heaven is a good father, your God, who has adopted you into His family forever. You no longer have to be afraid. Look at this verse and I invite you to memorize it when you forget who you really are.

> *For you did not receive a spirit of slavery to fall back into fear, but you received the spirit of adoption. When we cry "Abba, Father!" It is that very spirit bearing witness with our spirit that we are children of God. (Romans 8:15-16, NRSV)*

The word Abba actually means "Daddy." No father on earth is perfect, but your Father in heaven is perfect. He loves you passionately and sent Jesus to die for you. No matter what your experience with your earthly father has been (good or bad) you need to know that your Father in Heaven is infinitely good and will take care of you forever. Most people don't know that they have this kind of intimate relationship with God and that He has given them His authority and power. If it's true that God has given you power to shut up the Enemy, what's stopping you?

The Enemy might be lying to you right now saying stuff like, *Who do you think you are to do this? God sees the sinful stuff you're doing and He isn't going to give you power to do anything. God doesn't love you. God isn't real. The Enemy isn't real.* These are the kinds of lies the Enemy whispers all the time. Don't believe it! Shut up those lies. When you hear those lies or other dark thoughts, I want you to try something simple but powerful. Say to those bad voices in your head, "Shut up in Jesus' name! I belong to God. I am God's child."

Most of us need constant reminders about the truth of who we really are, because the Enemy will lie to us about our identity. One way to stand against the Enemy's lies is to declare God's truth from the Bible. You can do that by re-reading those Bible verses in chapter seven and claim those as truths about who you really are! Then, tell the Enemy to shut up.

4. Take out the garbage

Remember how we talked about our pain being like garbage? Sometimes, we need to "take out the garbage" that we are carrying around inside ourselves. We all have garbage in our lives. This can be stuff we are doing we know isn't good for us or stuff we might be doing that is hurting other people. Garbage can mean things like emotional wounds from abuse, bullying, or even pain that's buried deep inside our hearts. In fact, we might not even realize that garbage is there. Getting rid of the garbage in our lives is so important if we want to shut up those negative voices. The Enemy feeds on garbage like this, and it's important that you get rid of it. You can confess these sins and pain to God, and tell Him you want Him to come and wash you clean. Tell Him you want His healing. God's promise is to do just that. He will come and heal you of it.

In Hawaii, I was speaking to a large group of teenagers about God's love that can wash away any sin or mistake in our past. Afterward, I invited those who wanted to come up for prayer if they wanted to receive God's healing and forgiveness. One beautiful story I won't forget. A young boy (I'll call him Tim) came up to my friend Jason who was praying with guys. Tim said to Jason,

"I want God to forgive me, but the sin I'm doing makes me feel like God wouldn't ever love me again." Jason looked at the boy and gently invited him to share his secret sin. Tim looked at Jason and con- fessed he had been addicted to pornography. Tim said he couldn't do homework, leave the house or think about anything else other than porn. Jason started praying over Tim saying,

"Lord, we thank you that Tim is your son, a man of God. We renounce this sin of pornography and remember that you promise if we confess our sins, you will remove it as far as the east is from the west. So, Tim, I say to you in Jesus' name: You are forgiven. You are a man of God. This sin does not define you. God loves you completely. You are clean."

Tim began to weep and put his head on Jason's shoulder crying tears of joy. He left feeling clean, forgiven and free.

You don't need to live with garbage in your life. God can heal any shame, guilt, or emotional pain you're carrying around inside your heart.

Lastly, I want to encourage you that shutting up the negative and dark voices is easier if you don't remain alone in your pain. I know that it's hard to find people where you feel safe to share your pain and problems. The next chapter will help you think about how you can find some safe people who will shut up and listen.

WHAT DO YOU THINK?

x   Can you think of at least one lie you believe about yourself?

x   Did you try writing "shut up" in red over those names? How did that feel to you?

x   God can heal you and remove any garbage in your life. Is there "garbage" that you want gone from your life?

Note: It's powerful to share your garbage in a safe, small group of friends and then have them pray this prayer over you:

"Dear Jesus,

[NAME] has told us that [he/she] wants to get rid of this garbage in [his/her] life. We ask you now to cleanse [him/her] and remove it. Your word tells us in 1 John 1:9 that 'If we confess our sins, He is faithful and just and will forgive us our sins and purify us from all unrighteousness.' So, thank you that we can confess and get rid of garbage inside and You will cleanse us!"

CHAPTER 9

Find Safe People (Who Will Shut Up and Listen)

X   When Corey was a baby, I caught my father-in-law secretly feeding her grapefruit. Our pediatrician had recently told us that feeding a baby grapefruit isn't a great idea. The funny thing is that I had just told my father-in-law Pepaw not to feed Corey grapefruit, but he was doing it anyway. (Ha!) I adore my father-in-law (who now lives with Jesus in heaven), and I can't wait to see him again one day. Pepaw was a World War II veteran who fought in the battle of Iwo Jima, and he is one of the bravest men I will ever know in this life. Pepaw was also hilarious. So I wasn't surprised at his response when, with a twinkle in my eye, I said,

"Pepaw! Are you still feeding Corey that grapefruit I just told you not to feed her?" Pepaw looked up like he had been caught with his hand in the cookie jar, and he burst out laughing and said,

"Christy Anne! You are like the mother pig. When the mother pig sees someone going after her baby piglets, she charges them and they better watch out." I laughed and laughed. Pepaw was right. I've always been super protective of my kids. Hopefully people don't see me as a "mother pig" but I will always be a mom looking out for my kids and trying to keep them safe.

Even though I'm not your mom, I feel a great sense of responsibility for those of you who are reading this book. It takes courage to open up to anyone and share your problems. Not only that, it's hard to find safe people that you trust. You need to know that if you risk talking to people about your private pain, that they will actually help you and not harm you. Right?

Please allow me to be a little overprotective of you, even though you don't know me and I'm not your mom. While I don't know your exact problems and how to fix them, I can promise you that God knows and wants to help you. I can also promise you that staying alone and isolated when you're hurting will only harm you in the long run. If you were my kid, I would give you this advice: "Whatever it takes, whatever it costs, let's find some safe people you can trust who will listen and encourage you."

WHY DO YOU NEED SAFE PEOPLE?

God wants you to have safe people in your life that you can trust. Nobody can truly help you unless they are willing to *listen to you and compassionately understand your problems.* It can be scary to feel alone and that no one "gets it" when it comes to your life. The Enemy will always lie to you and try to make you think that you're completely alone. Other people can help you expose the lies inside your mind and remind you that your life is worth living. They can tell you the truth: You can be happy again.

I promise you that there really are safe people out there who will listen and help you. It may take some prayer and searching on your part, but safe people can be found. Safe people will listen to you, encourage you and help you expose those lies in your mind. They will speak loving truth that can change your life.

HOW DO YOU FIND SAFE PEOPLE WHO WILL SHUT UP AND LISTEN?

I've worked with enough teens and young adults to know this isn't simple or always easy. In fact, I have talked with hundreds of people about this very problem. They've given me many good reasons why they've made the choice to not talk with others about their problems. The majority of teens and young adults we've surveyed say they won't talk to a counselor because (a) they don't think a counselor will help, (b) they don't have the money, (c) the waiting lists are too long when they have tried in the past, (d) their parents won't let them, or (e) they're worried friends will think they are crazy if they see a counselor. In fact, very good therapists who are my friends admit that so many barriers exist between your generation's suffering and getting you the help you deserve.

So, what are your options? I'm going to give you some possible ideas about people who might be good candidates for a "safe person" in your life. I'm also going to share some online anonymous, safe coaching which allows you to share your pain with a trained counselor who can help you through texting, email, or phone calls. Finally, there are some good books and apps you can download which can be inspiring and might give you some hopeful life lines that will help you.

Right now, I would invite you to close your eyes and pray. Ask God to help you find the right safe people and resources that will help you. No person on this earth, not even your best friend, knows you or loves you like Jesus. God wants to see you healed, free, and happy. So just ask God to bring to your mind safe people who will help you hear God's voice and shut up the negative and dark voices. (If you don't hear anything, don't worry! Just read these ideas and trust your gut feeling about what's right for you.)

My husband, Ben, has a funny saying he says in a southern drawl that he learned growing up in Mississippi: "Chew up the fish, spit out the bones." That means that what helps one person might not help another person in life. Keep that in mind because I'm giving you 10 ideas of safe people and resources that might help you. (I trust you to figure out which ones are best for you!) But, you need discernment, right? You need to "chew up the fish and spit out the bones" and ask for God's help selecting the right safe people or resources for you. Who knows? As you read the choices below, you might decide that these aren't the best people to talk with, but God might whisper another idea in your head.

Who are safe people and/or what are some good resources that might be able to help me?

1. YOUR PARENTS

As a Mom, I always hope that if one of my kids is in trouble or hurting, that they would first come to me. My husband and I constantly emphasize to our kids that no matter what the problem is, we will love them. Corey, Annie, and Benji talk to me. Most of the time, I think they would tell you that I listen and love them, and will try to get them the help they need. I'm not perfect, and sometimes I won't know how to help. Only Jesus knows the exact things His kids need all the time.

Teens and college students will often tell me that they want to tell their parents but they don't want to be a burden. They may feel like their parents are already stressed (divorce, financial pressures, etc.) and they don't want to add to their stress. So, they stay alone and silent in their pain.

Most parents I know truly love their kids and want to help them but may be unaware of how much they are suffering and feel inadequate about how to help. It's possible that your parents would really care and help you if you opened up to them.

There are other parents, however, who are part of the problem. It's a sad reality today that some teens are being abused (either physical-ly, emotionally, or sexually) by a parent or relative. This is tragic, and it breaks God's heart. What is the definition of abuse? Here are some definitions of abuse and how you can recognize it. I would recom-mend you check out this website because it gives you definitions of abuse (which is never OK) regardless of whether it's a parent, teach-er, boyfriend, girlfriend, or anyone else. When abuse is going on, the teen or college student can sometimes believe that it's their fault. This is a lie. If you're being abused, it's the fault of the person abusing you. It's not because you deserve it. No one should be abused. Ever. You should be informed about what constitutes abuse and how to protect yourself. Here are some definitions from www.kidshealth.org, but I encourage you to check out the website for yourself, and follow what the doctors recommend if you are being abused.

Physical abuse is often the most easily recognized form of abuse. Physical abuse can be any kind of hitting, shaking, burning, pinching, biting, choking, throwing, beating, and other actions that cause physical injury, leave marks, or cause pain.

Sexual abuse is any type of sexual contact between an adult and anyone younger than 18; between a significantly older child and a younger child; or if one person overpowers another, regardless of age. If a family member sexually abuses another family member, this is called incest.

Emotional abuse can be the most difficult to identify because there are usually no outward signs of the abuse. Emotional abuse happens when yelling and anger go too far or when parents constantly criticize, threaten, or dismiss kids or teens until their self-esteem and feelings of self-worth are damaged. Emotional abuse can hurt and cause damage just as physical abuse does.

Recognizing Abuse

It may sound strange, but people sometimes have trouble recognizing that they are being abused. Recognizing abuse may be especially difficult for someone who has lived with it for many years. A person might think that it's just the way things are and that there's nothing that can be done. People who are abused might mistakenly think that it's their fault for not doing what their parents tell them, breaking rules, or not living up to someone's expectations.

Growing up in a family where there is violence or abuse can make a person think that is the right way or the only way for family members to treat each other. Somebody who has only known an abusive relationship might mistakenly think that hitting, beating, pushing, shoving, or angry name-calling are perfectly normal ways to treat someone when you're mad. Seeing parents treat each other in abusive ways might lead a child to think that's OK in relationships. But abuse is not a typical or healthy way to treat people. If you're not sure you are being abused, or if you suspect a friend is, it's always OK to ask a trusted adult or friend. [27]

If you feel afraid to talk with your parents, pray about it. If you're afraid of being punished or shamed for your feelings or problems, then maybe some of the people below could help you.

2. YOUR YOUTH PASTOR

Do you go to a church? If you do, are you connected with the youth pastor? Often, youth pastors are great people to confide in about your problems. They will listen and give you some good advice, and their job is to love you, not judge you. Their job is to pray with you and help you find God's healing and help. If you are at a college, some nationwide options for you to consider are Young Life, Navigators, Campus Crusade for Christ, and InterVarsity Christian Fellowship.

3. A KIND TEACHER YOU THINK WILL GET IT

Is there a teacher at your school who you feel connected with that seems safe and willing to listen? Often, teachers really care and will have good ideas or wisdom for you.

4. A DOCTOR OR COUNSELOR

Do you have a pediatrician or family doctor that you trust? I know my family is very close to our doctors! Do you have a family doctor who you like? When you speak to a doctor, everything is confidential so I would consider approaching them.

I know many of you don't trust counselors. That's OK. And I think it's good to be picky about who you're going to open up with to share your deepest hurts. Still, I want to encourage you that there are good counselors out there who can be very helpful. There are compassionate counselors who know how to handle depression, anxiety, eating disorders, cutting, sexual struggles, drug and alcohol addictions, and suicidal thoughts. They are trained to help and heal people from these things. Having said that, it's important to find the right person who is a good fit for you. If you think your parents would support you in finding a counselor, I would encourage you to ask them and try one. Sometimes your school will have a counselor on staff. It may be worth checking out. If you do try it out, I would encourage you to be very honest and real with your counselor, and if you don't feel he or she is helping you after you have given it a good few tries (sometimes you need to do a few times to know), get another counselor or keep reading for some other ideas. Don't feel trapped. Feel free to tell your parents I said that. You shouldn't be forced to stay with counselors that are pressuring you to do anything that makes you feel worse. It may take time to know for sure, but remember that the whole point of counseling is to be with an encouraging person who feels safe and can help you get better.

Lastly, I will tell you that many times, good medication can be helpful for teens and college students who are suffering from depression, anxiety, or suicidal thoughts. There is good medication out there that can truly be a lifesaver when it comes to depression, anxiety, and even sleeplessness. However, it's important that you find a good psychiatrist (the person who can prescribe medication like that) who is experienced treating adolescents because they need to carefully select and monitor any medication you start taking.

5. A FAMILY FRIEND OR RELATIVE THAT SEEMS SAFE

Maybe you have a family friend or relative that you have always felt loves you and accepts you no matter what. These are the people who make you feel good about yourself. These are the folks who feel safe. Sometimes, talking with these people can be a good first step before going to another adult. Can you think of someone?

6. ONLINE HELP FOR DEPRESSION, ANXIETY, SUICIDAL THOUGHTS, AND OTHER MENTAL HEALTH PROBLEMS

I know many of you want help, but would prefer to do it online yourself, without going to talk with someone in person. Here are some good options for you to check out. While they aren't substitutes for meeting with a good doctor, counselor, or psychiatrist in person, I think they could be very helpful to you:

mADAP (Adolescent Depression Awareness Program)
The Department of Psychiatry and Behavioral Sciences at Johns Hopkins has developed two new digital platforms to educate the public about mental health issues: a mobile app focused on teen depression and a website with video questions and answers about mood disorders. The app mADAP provides information and videos on identifying, diagnosing, and treating adolescent depression.

www.golantern.com
A friend of mine started a company called Lantern. Coaches who are trained in counseling are available online to talk with you about your problems. They are safe people who are trained to help, and this online organization is helping people all over the world. It's not a substitute for a personal counselor, but many teens and college students have been helped tremendously by Lantern. In fact, some

states have invested in buying a Lantern app for their college students who feel they need help with their problems. Check out this resource by going to www.golantern.com.

7. YOUR FRIENDS

Here is the good news and the bad news. Most teens and college students tell me that the person they're most likely to tell their problems to is a good friend. It's understandable. Good friends can seem like the best safe, non-judgmental people we may know. The bad news is that your friends will often not know how to best help you with your problems. They probably care, but they don't have the experience or resources to help you know what to do for healing and hope. Also, it can be very heavy if someone comes to you (or your friend) and shares he or she is depressed, cutting, doing drugs, suicidal, or have other problems. It can feel scary because once you know your friend's problem, then you can feel trapped, right? You don't want to break a friend's confidence by telling someone else what he or she confided to you. They may even have made you promise not to tell anyone. But that leaves you in a tough place, right? You might feel worried that your friend is in trouble. And it's terrible to be afraid they might get worse or even die. It's a very real problem many people face today.

My encouragement to you is this: If a friend comes to you and tells you about their pain, you don't have to carry that alone. I know it's tricky. You don't want to hurt them by telling someone else. At the same time, only God and other safe adults can really help. You can't carry that burden on your own, and you can't be responsible for a friend hurting himself or herself or someone else. If you're worried about someone, maybe you could give him or her a copy of this book. (If you can't afford a copy, let us know.) Hopefully, the ideas in this chapter might encourage your friend to connect to one of these other safe people or resources. If your friend won't listen, and you're concerned that he or she might do something dangerous, then really, you have no other choice but to tell an adult right away. It's not betraying your friend. It's actually being a good friend. Choosing to tell a safe adult might just save a life. You don't want to live with regrets, wishing you had told someone if a friend goes through with a suicidal plan. That's not fair to you or them. You could also tell them about the mADAP app and www.golantern.com (above) and the Crisis Text Line (see below). But do tell someone safe you trust who is an adult.

If you are the person who wants to tell your friend about your pain or problem, please don't ask another teen or young person to be solely responsible for carrying the burden of your problem. Communicate that you are also planning to tell a safe adult about your problem. That way, you are being a good friend and a safe place too.

8. CRISIS TEXT LINE (CTL)

Crisis Text Line serves anyone, in any time of crisis, providing access to free 24 hours a day, seven days a week support and information via the medium people already use and trust: text. Just text 741-741 from anywhere in the United States. A live, trained crisis counselor receives the text and responds quickly.

9. THE *SHUT UP* WEBSITE: WWW.SAYSHUTUP.COM

My daughter Corey loves to read but my daughter Annie isn't a big fan of books and would rather check out things online. Benji says he does both. I'm including our website here because all of these "Find Safe People" resources from this chapter are on our website. If you have friends you want to connect with help, they might prefer looking at our website instead of a book.

We have many resources available to you on our website at www.sayshutup.com. On the website, you can find videos of teens and college students talking about how they found help at times when they were sad, anxious, or feeling hopeless. The website will connect you to various videos on how to find healing for depression, anxiety, or other problems. You can also connect with me and my friends via email and you can request prayer at any time. If you have a friend who has just told you that he or she is planning to hurt himself or herself or someone else, there are ideas on what to do. Finally, there is a list of safe people to contact if you are in crisis.

10. *JESUS CALLING* APP

Many teens and college students have told me that they've found inspiration and encouragement through the *Jesus Calling* books and app. Millions of people have had their lives impacted by the encouraging words of Sarah Young in the best-selling, 365-day devotional, *Jesus Calling*. You can order this book online, get it in most bookstores or download the *Jesus Calling* app.

IF YOU'RE IN CRISIS RIGHT NOW....

If you are considering hurting yourself or someone else right now, then I want you to tell an adult right away, text CTL at 741-741 and if you can't reach anyone, please go to the nearest emergency room.

GOD SEES YOU AND YOU ARE LOVED

As you finish reading this book, I want to leave you with this final thought: God sees you. You may feel alone sometimes and think that no one understands the real you, but God does. You are seen and loved by the God of the Universe who knows your name. God has the answers to all of your pain and problems, and you really can learn to hear God's voice. Remember my promise at the start of this book? I told you that I wouldn't pretend that there are always easy answers to every problem. The truth is this: There is only One person you can count on to always be safe, accepting, and loving no matter what. That's Jesus Christ. You can experience the presence of Jesus and His unconditional love through the Holy Spirit. This God is love, and when He sees you, His heart is filled with compassion for you. As you put your faith in Him, His promise is that He will never leave you alone or abandon you. So, as you finish reading, I want to remind you one last time: You are God's special kid. You have His power to **shut up** any voice that's trying to tear you down. You are strong in God's mighty power. You are an overcomer, and God has a wonderful plan for your future.

YOUR FUTURE WITH GOD

"For I know the plans I have for you," declares the Lord, "plans to prosper you and not to harm you, plans to give you a hope and a future." (Jeremiah 29:11, NIV)

He gives power to the weak and strength to the powerless. Even youths will become weak and tired, and young men (and women) will fall in exhaustion. But those who trust in the Lord will find new strength. They will soar high on wings like eagles. They will run and not grow weary. They will walk and not faint. (Isaiah 40:29-31, NLT)

MORE THAN CONQUERORS

What, then, shall we say in response to these things? If God is for us, who can be against us? He who did not spare his own Son, but gave him up for us all—how will he not also, along with him, graciously give us all things? Who will bring any charge against those whom God has chosen? It is God who justifies. Who then is the one who condemns? No one. Christ Jesus who died—more than that, who was raised to life—is at the right hand of God and is also interceding for us. Who shall separate us from the love of Christ? Shall trouble or hardship or persecution or famine or nakedness or danger or sword? As it is written:

> *"For your sake we face death all day long;*
> *we are considered as sheep to be slaughtered."*

No, in all these things we are more than conquerors through him who loved us. For I am convinced that neither death nor life, neither angels nor demons, neither the present nor the future, nor any powers, neither height nor depth, nor anything else in all creation, will be able to separate us from the love of God that is in Christ Jesus our Lord. (Romans 8:31–39, NIV)

WHAT DO YOU THINK?

x   As you finish this book, and consider safe people who might help you or a friend, what do you think? Do you know safe people that you can really talk to about your problems?

x   Do you have friends who could use this book, the www.sayshutup.com website, or the *God is Whispering to You* book? Please have them contact us if they want a copy but can't afford one at info@sayshutup.com.

x   Which of the options in this chapter might you consider checking out that you haven't used before?

x   Do you feel "seen" by God? Do you know how loved you are?

Appendix

Get a **FREE** download of chapters one through three of this book for a friend at www.sayshutup.com.

A **FREE** download of chapters one through three of the book *Broken Treasures* can be found here: www.crackedeggministries.com

A **FREE** download of chapters one through three of Christy's other book, *God is Whispering to You*, can be found here: www.christypierce.org

Notes

PREFACE

1   Melonie Heron, *Deaths: Leading Causes for 2013*, National Vital Statistics Reports 65, no 2 (Hyattsville, MD: National Center for Health Statistics, 2016), 10, accessed August 1, 2016, http://www.cdc.gov/nchs/data/nvsr/nvsr65/nvsr65_02.pdf.

2   "Suicide Prevention: Youth Suicide," Centers for Disease Control and Prevention, last modified March 10, 2015, accessed July 26, 2016, www.cdc.gov/ViolencePrevention/suicide/youth_suicide.html.

3   Ibid.

4   *Depression in Children and Adolecents Fact Sheet* (Bethesda, MD: National Institute of Mental Health, 2012),1, accessed August 1, 2016, http://www.teachmeceus.com/material/Depression%20in%20Children,%20Adolescents,%20and%20Young%20Adults.pdf.

5   "Two Chinese Teens Commit Suicide Over Unfinished Homework, Says Report," 2013, *indiatoday*, May 4, accessed July 27, 2016, http://indiatoday.intoday.in/story/two-chinese-teens-commit-suicide-over-unfinished-homework-says-report/1/269192.html.

6   Will Englund, "Teens Choosing Death in Russia," 2012, *The Washington Post*, March 7, accessed July 27, 2016, https://www.washingtonpost.com/world/europe/teens-choosing-death-in-russia/2012/03/01/gIQADrhPwR_story.html.

7   American College Health Association, 14.

8   Heron, *Deaths: Leading Causes for 2013*.

INTRODUCTION

9   "Let Them Sleep: AAP Recommends Delaying Start Times of Middle and High Schools to Combat Teen Sleep Deprivation," American Academy of Pediatrics, August 25, 2014, accessed August 1, 2016, https://www.aap.org/en-us/about-the-aap/aap-press-room/pages/let-them-sleep-aap-recommends-delaying-start-times-of-middle-and-high-schools-to-combat-teen-sleep-deprivation.aspx#sthash.3MokLw6e.dpuf.

10   Ibid.

CHAPTER 1

11   Sarra L. Hedden, Joel Kennet, Rachel Lipari, Grace Medley, and Peter Tice, *Behavioral Health Trends in the United States: Results from the 2014 National Survey on Drug Use and Health* (Rockville, MD: Center for Behavioral Health Statistics and Quality, Substance Abuse and Mental Health Services Adminstration, 2015), accessed August 1, 2016, http://www.samhsa.gov/data/sites/default/files/NSDUH-FRR1-2014/NSDUH-FRR1-2014.htm.

12   American College Health Association, 14.

13   University of Michigan, "Students with Depression Twice as Likely to Drop Out of College," ScienceDaily, last modified July 7, 2009, accessed August 1, 2016, https://www.sciencedaily.com/releases/2009/07/090706161302.htm.

14   American College Health Association, 14.

CHAPTER 2

15   Ruthann Richter, 2015, "Go to Bed: Social and School Pressures Prompt Many Stressed Teens to Forsake Sleep," *Stanford Medicine Magazine*, Fall 2015, accessed July 27, 2016, http://stanmed.stanford.edu/2015fall/go-to-bed.html.

16 Lairs Johnson, "Teen Takes Her Life After 'Friends' Posted Pictures on Snapchat," To Save A Life, accessed July 26, 2016, http://www.tosavealife.com/teen-takes-life-friends-posted-pictures-snapchat/.

CHAPTER 4

17 "Teen Depression," National Institute of Mental Health, accessed August 2, 2016, http://www.nimh.nih.gov/health/publications/teen-depression/index.shtml.

18 Kevin Egan, Ellen Bara Stolzenberg, Joseph J. Ramirez, Melissa C. Aragon, Maria Ramirez Suchard, and Sylvia Hurtado, *The American Freshman: National Norms Fall 2014* (Los Angeles: Higher Education Research Institute, UCLA, 2014), 13, accessed August 8, 2016, http://www.heri.ucla.edu/monographs/theamericanfreshman2014.pdf.

19 American College Health Association, 14.

20 Amy Novotney, "Students Under Pressure," *Monitor* 45, no. 8 (September 2014): 36, accessed July 27, 2016, http://www.apa.org/monitor/2014/09/cover-pressure.aspx. Reprinted with permission.

21 Ibid.

CHAPTER 5

22 "Youth Bullying: What Does the Research Say?" Centers for Disease Control and Prevention, last modified July 12, 2016, accessed August 18, 2016, http://www.cdc.gov/violenceprevention/youthviolence/bullyingresearch/.

23 R. Matthew Gladden, Alana M. Vivolo-Kantor, Merle E. Hamburger, and Corey D. Lumpkin, *Bullying Surveillance Among Youths: Uniform Definitions for Public Health and Recommended Data Elements, Version 1.0* (Atlanta, GA; National Center for Injury Prevention and Control, Centers for Disease Control and Prevention and U.S. Department of Education, 2013) accessed August 18, 2016, http://www.cdc.gov/violenceprevention/pdf/bullying-definitions-final-a.pdf.

24 Corinne David-Ferdon and Marci Feldman Hertz, *Electronic media and youth violence: A CDC Issue Brief for Researchers* (Atlanta, GA: Centers for Disease Control and Prevention and U.S. Department of Health and Human Services; 2009) accessed August 18, 2016, http://www.cdc.gov/ViolencePrevention/pdf/Electronic_Aggression_Researcher_Brief-a.pdf.

CHAPTER 6

25 "Democratic Republic of the Congo," World Without Genocide, accessed August 18, 2016, http://worldwithoutgenocide.org/genocides-and-conflicts/congo.

26 Richard Gallagher, 2016, "As a Psychiatrist, I Diagnose Mental Illness. Also, I Help Spot Demon Possession," *The Washington Post*, July 1, accessed August 2, 2016, https://www.washingtonpost.com/posteverything/wp/2016/07/01/as-a-psychiatrist-i-diagnose-mental-illness-and-sometimes-demonic-possession/.

CHAPTER 9

27 "What is Abuse?" *The Nemours Foundation/KidsHealth®,* accessed July 28, 2016, http://kidshealth.org/en/teens/family-abuse.html. Reprinted with permission.

Notebook